"Unseen Footsteps of Jesus"

OLAM HABA

(Future World)

Mysteries Book 1-"Pre-Dawn"

JERRY AYERS

author**HOUSE**

AuthorHouse™
1663 Liberty Drive
Bloomington, IN 47403
www.authorhouse.com
Phone: 833-262-8899

© 2023 Jerry Ayers. All rights reserved.

No part of this book may be reproduced, stored in a retrieval system, or transmitted by any means without the written permission of the author.

Published by AuthorHouse 02/01/2023

ISBN: 978-1-7283-7804-6 (sc)
ISBN: 978-1-7283-7802-2 (hc)
ISBN: 978-1-7283-7803-9 (e)

Library of Congress Control Number: 2023901774

Print information available on the last page.

Any people depicted in stock imagery provided by Getty Images are models, and such images are being used for illustrative purposes only.
Certain stock imagery © Getty Images.

This book is printed on acid-free paper.

Because of the dynamic nature of the Internet, any web addresses or links contained in this book may have changed since publication and may no longer be valid. The views expressed in this work are solely those of the author and do not necessarily reflect the views of the publisher, and the publisher hereby disclaims any responsibility for them.

CONTENTS

Chapter 1 1
Chapter 2 4
Chapter 3 14
Chapter 4 24
Chapter 5 32
Chapter 6 42
Chapter 7 57
Chapter 8 69
Chapter 9 86
Chapter 10 105
Chapter 11... 117
Chapter 12 129
Chapter 13 141
Chapter 14... 155
Chapter 15 167
Chapter 16... 182

1

Yahuah Yahusha (the Creator) looked down from His heavenly abode at the growing darkness covering His earthly creation. It seemed as though the satanic nightfall would forever darken the Sunrise of the east in the land of Yhuwdah (Judah). It is now 334 B.C., one-thousand and thirteen years since He had promised this land to Abraham and his descendents. At that time in 2147 B.C. his name was still Abram, meaning 'high father'. However, later Yahuah Yahusha changed his name to Abraham meaning 'father of a multitude'. Now the Greeks under the leadership of Alexander the Great, the son of Philip from Macedonia had taken control of this covenant land promised to the Hebrews. The pagan Greek practices of satanic idolatry filled the heavens with the stench of a hellish death. Yet, Yahuah Yahusha knew it was not time for the Sunrise on High to appear in the dawning of Light for the Hebrew nation because they did not have their calloused hearts turned in full allegiance towards Him.

Elsewhere in the world Yahuah Yahusha would have to wait for the eleven-year-old *Imperium Romanum*, Roman Empire, to continue to gain strength in the city of Rome as it contended with the other Latin tribes to gain world power. Rome first had to control most of Europe and the Mediterranean area before Yahuah Yahusha could use this soon-to-be-great city against Satan's plan of mankind's eternal destruction. Sinister evil begat more evil as the pungent stench of satanic power oozed from the dark governmental powers of Hellenistic (Greek) rule and the birthing of Latin dominance. Even though a thick spiritual darkness was permeating the Yahuah-given domain of mankind by satanic excretion, the human heart whether it be Hebrew, Greek, Roman or other pagan types across the entire globe was not ready to yield to Yahusha, meaning *salvation*.

Satanic darkness grew darker and darker as the Greek and Latin powers grew stronger. Then in 167 B.C., demonic bestial hissing heralded like a public crier, intruded into the ever listening ears of Yahuah Yahusha. What was Satan conjuring up in his cauldron of death and destruction? It was at this moment that Yahuah Yahusha saw the abomination by the actions of the Greek ruler Antiochus IV Epiphanes as he desecrated the Sacred Temple of Yahuah Yahusha. Antiochus IV Epiphanes set up an altar as a figure of a dragon to the false idol god Zeus in the Holy of Holies of the Temple of Yruwshalaim (Jerusalem) and spilled the blood of swine on it for sacrificial offerings to this Greek god. He also forbade the circumcision rites of the Hebrews under the penalty of death for disobedience. The parents and infants were barbarically slaughtered and then their bodies burned with flames of fire like the swine in a holocaust offering to satisfy the craving for blood of the Hellenistic god Zeus. Their agonizing screams, rivers of thick red blood and gray ashes that fell from the sky like snow from their charred bodies lit a small flicker of fire in the hard hearts of the Hebrews.

Yes, Yahuah Yahusha could see a faint flicker of a flame in the hearts of the Hebrew people. They were finally going to turn their hearts to Him and stand up against this power of darkness causing death and destruction being conjured up in the demonic cauldron of Satan. Finally, the beginning flicker of a pre-dawn light began to break this darkness of eternal damnation against the Hebrew people and all of mankind. Who would answer the call of Yahuah Yahusha to fan the flame of this flicker of light against the putrid darkness of

Satan's demonic destruction? Was there a righteous Hebrew left in the land who would not bow the knee to the imposturous Hellenistic god and its master in Greece? Did mankind finally have hope to usher in the restoration of eternal fellowship with Yahuah Yahusha? Then out of the shadows of the deep darkness stepped forward a righteous man from the little valley village of Modi'im who had the heart of a relentless warrior for the kingdom of Yahuah.

The black bestial demon of death and destruction conjured up in the cauldron of Satan spread his wings, set his fangs and extended his blood thirsty talons towards the innocent little village of Modi'im. He flew swiftly from the great city of Yruwshalaim with his long narrow tongue panting for more innocent blood with each stroke of his giant blackish wings. What could stop this creature of extreme darkness? Was there any hope?

2

The little village of Modi'im was nestled in a small valley between Yruwshalaim and Yafo (Joppa). It was twenty-two miles southeast of the port city of Yafo and nineteen miles west of Yruwshalaim. Being located on the main highway leading from Yruwshalaim to the sea port city of Yafo it was known as the gateway to the great Mediterranean Sea. White limestone clefts jutted out of the hills three miles to the north of the village creating the illusion of snow packed hills. However, the hills just two miles to the south of the village were dotted with towering green fir trees.

This narrow valley between the northern and southern hills provided the little village of Modi'im lush and fertile soil for its important commerce. Its dusty roads were well traveled with the coming and going to the port city of Yafo or to the capital city of Yruwshalaim. No matter how important the business of the travelers coming and going was they always had to stop in this little village to purchase some of its produce. The valley floor just outside the little village was lined with perfect rows of lush grapevines. These grapevines produced some of the finest wine being exported to the west from the seaport of Yafo headed to far off lands across the Mediterranean Sea or the wine was sold to the east in the souks in the great city of Yruwshalaim. This fine wine soothed the parched throats of the weary travelers as they took a brief respite from their comings and goings through this gateway village.

Modi'im's fine wine didn't get all the attention of the commercial trade because in the rest of the surrounding valley and on its hills to the south could be heard the ever bleating of large goat herds. These multi-colored herds of brown, black and whites were transformed onto the canvas of the hides of these shaggy animals and appeared in solid colors, stripped and even speckled patterns. The large goat herds provided this little gateway village with its other important commerce of tasty cheese and tantalizing curds. Weary and hungry travelers could not resist these products and satisfied their aching hunger pangs with a stomach full of the variety of these cheeses and of course were being washed down with the village's fine wine.

Yet, even though the revenue generated from the vast grapevines and large goat herds was important to the little village of Modi'im being located on the dusty road of the main port highway from the capital city, it contained a little known secret. Its commerce of trade was not what made this little village in the valley most famous of all. The synagogue of Modi'im produced some of the finest and most important *kohen*, priests, in the history of the Hebrew people. The blood thirsty talons of Satan's hideous demonic beast of death and destruction conjured up in his evil cauldron could not seem to penetrate into the heart of this line of *kohen* from the village of Modi'im.

In the year of 167 B.C. in the little gateway village of Modi'im lived *hakohen,* the priest, named Matityahu ben Yowchanan (John) of the Maccabim family. He was the son of Yowchanan Maccabim and the grandson of Shim'own (Simeon) Maccabim and the great-grandson of Asmon. Therefore, his family was called Hashmonayim or translated meaning 'of the family of Asmon'. His great-grandfather Asmon was of the Hebrew priestly lineage of the tribal branch of Leviy. Asmon was the fifth grandson of Ida'Yah, the son of Yoarib, who was the grandson of Yachin. Yachin was a descendant of the third *HaGadowl Kohen*, high priest, Piynchac, the son of El'azar and the grandson of Aharown (Aaron) the brother of Mosheh (Moses) who led the Hebrews out of the closed fist of slavery in the land of Mitsrayim (Egypt).

Matityahu Maccabim had just completed his teaching in the synagogue of Modi'im when the doors shook violently and burst wide open with a great thunderous noise. In the now open doorway stood the figure of a young man bending at the waist with his hands on his knees breathing very hard. His body shook and was drenched with perspiration and his clothing covered with the chalky dust of the highway road of the valley. Over the loud panting of the young man in the open doorway of the synagogue Matityahu said in a commanding voice, "What is the meaning of this?" The young man caught his breath and said, "*Shalom Kohen*. Forgive me for my intrusion on your teaching but I have urgent news from the Temple in Yruwshalaim." Matityahu still a bit bewildered over the sudden intrusion quipped, "What could be so urgent from Yruwshalaim that you interrupt the synagogue? Have the Hellenes (Greeks) withdrawn back to the dog houses of their home country."

The breathless young man responded to Matityahu, "Not at all *Kohen*, just the opposite. I am Yitshar, the servant of *HaGadowl Kohen*, High Priest, Azaryah who has sent me with the urgent news." Matityahu growing impatient with young Yitshar blasted, "Go ahead boy. Quit beating around the bush and tell us of this urgent news before we all fly away to *Olam Haba*, the world to come, for the reason of old age!" Yitshar gathered himself with a short pause and replied, "The Hellenes have installed an idol figure of a dragon in the Most Sacred Place (Holy of Holies) of the Temple and dedicated it to their pagan god Zeus. They are spilling the blood of swine upon its altar and ordering the *kohen* in the city to do the same as a blood sacrifice to the supreme god of Hellenism. The chief Helene (Greek) in Yruwshalaim has even passed a law that we are no longer allowed to circumcise our baby *bens,* sons, and the punishment for disobedience will be the sacrifice of the parents and the baby *ben* on the dragon altar to quiet the wrath of Zeus."

The stunned audience of the synagogue was deathly silent and the aged and highly respected *koen,* Matityahu Maccabim fixed his intent gaze upon the young messenger, Yitshar, and said, "Now slow down Yitshar. May it never be! Start from the beginning and tell us what has happened in full detail. Someone, fetch the young man a drink of water and bread for nourishment. We must listen intently and learn all of what has happened." Then some women from the gallery of the synagogue rushed out to get young Yitshar some bread and water. After they had returned and Yitshar had satisfied his thirst and became refreshed from the nourishment of the bread, he began from the beginning the story of the abomination.

"You see honorable *kohen* and brothers of Modi'im, as you already know thirty-three years ago in 200 B.C. the Hellene Antiochus The Great had reasoned within himself to rule two kingdoms, his kingdom of Syria and also the kingdom of Mitsrayim (Egypt) which included the territory of Yhuwdah (Judah). Therefore, he entered into Mitsrayim with a great multitude of chariots, elephants, large ranks of horseman, a great army of foot soldiers with spears and swords and a vast navy of ships. The king of Mitsrayim melted with great fear when he saw this attack and fled from Antiochus The Great. Thus we became under the rule of the Antiochus family. His son Antiochus IV Epiphanes, which means 'God Manifest', who has ruled over us since 175 B.C has made our lives miserable over the past eight years."

"The past week he marched his strong warriors into the city of

Yruwshalaim and he proudly entered into the Temple and carried away its glorious vessels into captivity. He removed and took away from the Most Sacred Place (Holy of Holies) the golden altar along with the golden Mnowrah Chandelier lamp stand, the table of the show-bread, the pouring vessels, vials, censers, golden ornaments and the crowns. He also took away the silver, gold and hidden treasures which he found. His men slaughtered women and infants in the streets and mixed their blood as it flowed freely with the blood of our young men who were slain by the sword. He was heard boasting loudly as he rode off back to Syria that he had murdered in a massacre 185,000 men, women and children. Just before he left he ordered the image of the dragon of Zeus to be placed in the Most Sacred Place and to sacrifice swine on it, spilling their blood all over the temple."

"He has left word to his commanders in the city that all his kingdoms will be of one people and he will be their god and we are to follow his laws. Our sanctuary of the Temple has been laid to waste like a wilderness. He has forbidden our burnt-offerings to Yahuah and no longer can we present sacrifices and drink offerings in the Temple. We are to profane the Sabbaths and holy festival days set aside to worship Yahuah. We are even to eat unclean things and defile our bodies. In addition to these things, we are commanded to leave our *bens*, sons, uncircumcised and make their souls abominable with all manner of uncleanness and profanity. Those who are found in disobedience of his laws will be punished with death."

"Just this morning, the Hellene commanders and their soldiers rounded up the parents of circumcised *bens*, sons and took them inside the Temple to the altar of the dragon of Zeus. The men's blood was spilled as their women and children watched their men be slaughtered and offered as a sacrifice to Zeus. Next, the baby bens, sons, were placed on the altar of the dragon and their beating hearts were removed from their chest cavities as their mothers screamed in horror and agony. The remaining children of the families were systematically selected, their throats cut and their lifeless bodies spewing blood were thrown on the carcasses of dead swine. Then some of the soldiers had their way with the women before they also were slaughtered and their blood splattered on the walls of the sanctuary. The lifeless infant *bens*, sons, were taken back to their homes and hung by the necks with their open hollow chest cavities and hung from the doorways after the houses of disobedience had been ransacked."

Upon hearing this, Matityahu Maccabim and the men of the synagogue tore their clothes and plucked at their beards in great mourning as the women in the balcony wailed with great grief. The sun was beginning to set in the west but no one left the synagogue of teaching as it was turned into a house of extreme sorrow and great mourning. Yitshar, the young messenger remained with them in the synagogue throughout the night.

Now the pre-dawn light began to trickle into the still open doorway of the synagogue. There was little stirring as everyone was exhausted from the mental torture of extreme grief and unbearable sorrow of the unpleasant news that Yitshar had shared with the congregation the previous day. Slowly the loud cry of a hungry infant woke others from their horrific sleep and the congregation began to file out of the synagogue and head to their own homes. Matityahu and his five sons remained alone with Yitshar just outside the doorway of the synagogue of the little village Modi'im. Commerce trade from the products of grapevines and large goat herds were not on the minds of this family. Instead, the brewing of a great spiritual battle was stirring in the minds of this righteous Hebrew family.

Matityahu blessed Yitshar and prayed for travel safety back to the capital city of Yruwshalaim and before he sent him on his way he said, "Thank you for coming. We will be in vigilant prayer and seek the wisdom of Yahuah as we deal with this dreadful news. Tell Azaryah we will come soon to Yruwshalaim with council and do not fear the swords of men but only the wrath of the Almighty Yahuah!" After this, Yitshar the young servant of Azaryah *HaGadowl Kohen*, the High Priest, began down the dusty road east towards Yruwshalaim. Matityahu Maccabim and his five sons watched Yitshar until he was out of sight.

Matityahu looked at his five strong sons beside him as they stood staring fixed on a figure that had long walked out of their sight. Next to him was his oldest, Yowchanan (John) who was called 'Caddis', then Shim'own (Simon) who was called 'Thassi', and Yhuwdah (Judas) who was called Maccabi, and El'azar who was called 'Avaran' and finally Yownathan (Jonathan) whose surname was 'Apphus'. Each son had his strengths and also their weaknesses, yet as a group his sons were a formidable force to be reckoned with. He was proud of them, yet was unsure of the journey awaiting them. Matityahu stepped in front of them and said, "Sons, soon we will have to travel to Yruwshalaim to see the blasphemies that were committed in our Father's House. Come on, let's go home. Your mother is waiting with breakfast."

The nineteen miles back east to Yruwshalaim seemed to take longer and was much further today than it was yesterday. Yitshar felt very nervous and uneasy inside as if he was being followed. Yet, each time he turned around the road behind him was empty. This was strange. No travelers on such a busy main highway going to the sea port city of Yafo. His steps quickened as he got nearer and could see the outline of the great city at a far distance. Unknown to Yitshar, above him soared with flapping blackish wings the blood thirsty and hideous demonic beast of death and destruction of Satan which he conjured up in his evil cauldron. The beast's hollow black eyes were locked on Yitshar waiting for the perfect moment to devour him. The hideous creature could sense fear in Yitshar. The timing was right, the beast's victim was ripe for the picking. The hideous creature of darkness let out a blood curdling screeching sound that pierced the spiritual realm, extended its sharp talons and began a nosedive to attack the unknowing young servant of the *HaGadowl Kohen*, the High Priest.

It was mid-afternoon and Yitshar could see the towering western gates of the city of Yruwshalaim, so he began to sing a song of joy to drive out the fear. At that moment just as the hideous creature from the pits of hell was about to set its sharp talons into the heart of Yitshar a rotating flaming sword quickly made a swipe between the blood-thirsty beast and the young servant. The hideous beast tumbled out of control as the current of air and blinding light of the rotating sword glanced the side of the blackish monster. The hideous beast met the dusty earth of the highway with a great thud letting out a muffled whimper. It got back up refusing to go near the bright light of the rotating sword. The beast of darkness slowly began to flap its blackish wings and return back to the evil cauldron of Satan.

Yitshar quickly turned around and was met with a cloud of dust blowing down the deserted road. He covered his eyes and mouth until the dust quickly blew by. As he approached the west wall of the great city he would enter through the Yeshenah Gate next to the Pool of Amygdalon and then travel to the Upper City. Then it was just down the cobbled street to the well furnished house of Azaryah. When he had entered the Gennath Gate his chest was met with two sharp points of spear blades inching up towards his tender throat. A gruff voice bellowed, "What's your business here and what is your name boy!" His eyes focused and recognized that this rude welcome was the result of two Hellene (Greek) soldiers. In a soft muffled voice Yitshar answered the man, "I am Yitshar, the young servant of Azaryah, *HaGadowl Kohen,* the High Priest of the Temple of Yahuah." "You mean the temple of the powerful and almighty Zeus, don't you?" responded the second soldier. Without hesitating Yitshar said, "Azaryah is my master and I am late with a return message." *'Oh no what have I just done,'* he thought silently.

The interrogation began at that moment by the soldiers. "Where have you been and what message are you returning." Yitshar tried his best to get out of a bad situation responding, "It is of a private matter of Azaryah from the small village of Modi'im." "What? You come from Modi'im and do not return with fine wine or tasty cheese?" said the gruff soldier. The second soldier pressed the point of his spear into the throat of Yitshar drawing blood from the cut. Then the second soldier said, "I think he is lying and trying to make a fool of us." The first soldier became irritated with the situation and commanded, "You. You swine will be taken to the commander to get the truth out of you. Now march you stench of garbage!" At that moment, the hideous beast turned its head, hesitated and began to turn back around before it dove into the depths of the evil cauldron of Satan. Instantly, a flash of light met its hollow eyes and a whirling wind caught it wings driving it back into the deep dark depths of Satan's cauldron of demise.

After a thorough interrogation and investigation of Yitshar's absence and return to the great city by the Hellene (Greek) commander of armies, Yitshar was determined to be no threat to the well being of the sovereignty of the Hellenistic Empire. However, after Yitshar was released to go to the house of Azaryah, the commander and his officers decided it might be worth it to investigate further into this

Matityahu Maccabim living in the small valley village of Modi'im. Why was it important for the High Priest to send his private servant to deliver a personal message to this villager? What political power did this Matityahu of Modi'im possess if any? Maybe, just maybe he could be a powerful ally in dealing with subjugating these stubborn Hebrew people. This could mean a promotion or a large financial reward to a certain Hellene army commander so far away from his family back in Macedonia. Yes, a ticket out of this forsaken place and away from the stench of these forsaken Hebrew people. An unexpected visit to the little valley village of Modi'im was a must.

3

Thick pitch-black smoke billowed from the evil cauldron of Satan. Winds of evil blew over the cauldron and drifted purposefully towards the city of Yruwshalaim carrying with them the thick pitch-black smoke from Satan's evil cauldron. Eerie growling accompanied with hideous screaming came from within that cloud of evil darkness. As the darkness reached Yruwshalaim it hovered over the great city as a hunter would patiently circle its prey. Was Yruwshalaim the target of another evil disaster against Yahuah Yahusha? What more could happen to this once great Hebrew city? Was Satan finally going to claim and take full possession of this religious center of the world as his own? Just what was lurking in that thick cloud of evil darkness making such hideous and eerie sounds that seemed to stir the souls of the damned dead? Then a contriving hissing sound projected itself towards the Helene (Greek) military command headquarters.

At that very moment, the Helene (Greek) commander, Hippokrates, who was left in charge of the city of Yruwshalaim by King Antiochus IV Epiphanes, summoned his sergeant and commanded him to ready a squad of twenty men in full battle armor and stand to be ready to travel to the village of Modi'im. His sergeant entered the room and saluted his commander. "Are the troops about assembled?" asked Hippokrates. "As you commanded sir, are your going to ride your stallion or would you like your chariot made ready since dark clouds are in the sky sir?" asked the sergeant. Hippokrates strolled across the room towards the window to peer into the sky.

After reaching the window he intently gazed into the sky and then looked towards the western horizon in the direction of the village of Modi'im, his destination to carry out his devious and self-serving scheme. He rubbed both sides of his protruding chin with his thumb and forefinger of his right hand for a brief moment, scratched the top of his clean shaven head and then with a sly smile he spun on his heels and faced the sergeant saying, "Get old Hercules saddled. May Zeus control his thunderbolts today as the horizon towards Modi'im seems to be a clear sky. The dark clouds are just a passing storm and nothing for us to concern ourselves with." "As you wish sir," the sergeant said as he once again saluted and left the room closing the wooden door behind himself.

The bright morning rays of light from the dawning sun were met with clouds of sorrow as Matityahu Maccabim, his sons and the leading men of the city of Modi'im sat beside the dusty highway leading to Yruwshalaim on the east and Yafo to the west. They were all dressed in sackcloth of mourning and threw dust upon their heads as they prayed and wept for the Hebrew people in the great city of Yruwshalaim. Travelers on the dusty road would pass by shaking their heads and then would lift their eyes towards the heavens as if to silently implore Yahuah Yahusha to hear the prayers of these mighty men of the little village of Modi'im. Yowchanan (John) the eldest son of Matityahu glanced towards Yruwshalaim, then back to his father and said, "*Ab, ab,* Father, father, dark storm clouds are brewing over Yruwshalaim in the east. Should we also pray for protection from this storm to protect the grapevines from the winds and for the goat-herders to keep the large flocks together during the thunder and lightning?" Matityahu peered to the east then back to Yowchanan, "May the rays of light here chase away that storm in the east, lift your voice to Yahuah as you see fit."

As Hippokrates rode regally on the broad back of Hercules, the powerful black stallion, he inspected the five columns of four soldiers arrayed in full battle armor riding on brown cavalry trained horses. Their neatly combed manes ruffled slightly from the gentle breeze at their backs. Their tails switched from side to side in the attempt to shoo away any flies who might just want a friendly bite of horse flesh. They had traveled ten miles west of Yruwshalaim, yet it seemed as though the storm clouds were following them at their heels. Hippokrates gently nudged Hercules in the sides and Hercules responded with a soft trot to the front of the cavalry squadron. Hippokrates steered Hercules with his black shimmering muscles that rippled with each trotting hoof beat next to the horse of Sergeant Lycus and signaled for the squadron to proceed at a fast trot stirring up dust as they passed travelers on the road to Modi'im. Commander Hippokrates turned his head to the left towards Sergeant Lycus and said, "Let's speed up the matters of the business for the day. I think the storm clouds are following us!" "I hope even Zeus himself obeys your commands and withholds the thunder and lightning to keep our heads dry," jokingly said Sergeant Lycus.

Commander Hippokrates was correct in his observation of the dark storm clouds following them from the great city of Yruwshalaim. However, he was not aware of the evil lurking in these clouds as they did not contain thunder and lightning from Zeus but rather sinister death and destruction from Satan. The unseen bestial demons were like caged wild animals gnarling, growling and hissing wanting nothing more than to viciously attack and to tear to shreds unsuspecting innocent prey. In the midst of theses storm clouds raged two hideous beasts. One was in the appearance of a pitch-black ravenous hyena with long blood stained fangs protruding from its mouth. Its eyes were glowing red and its ribcage showed as thin flesh covered its gaunt midsection. Just above the ribcage were attached two slim folded wings. The tongue of the hyena dripped saliva as it impatiently paced back and forth across the slowly west moving clouds. The other beast was in the appearance of a large black gorilla with a large flat forehead, glowing red eyes were narrowly placed and set apart by only a short snout with two large nostril holes that shot forth a fog of smoke as the great beast exhaled. Its mouth was full of dark brown stained sharp teeth capable of ripping the throat of any prey in one bite. The gorilla's barrel chest and large belly was supported by two massive long arms and two large legs that were the size of tree trunks. On its back were two half-folded black broad wings. The gorilla sat still emitting a low growling sound as it clinched and unclenched its massive hands into evil murderous fists.

Yownathan (Jonathan) Maccabim nudged his older brother Yowchanan (John) pointing towards the east, "The black clouds of the storm in the east are getting closer and darker." Yowchanan looked up noting, "You are right brother. Look at that rising dust storm about two miles down the road." Matityahu heard his sons' conversation and gazed towards the east. Then he exclaimed, *"Rasha!* (Moral wrong!) Hurry everyone gather yourselves and change your clothes because we are about to have guests!" All the men scattered to their homes to remove the sackcloth and to put on their everyday robes as the cavalry squadron and the evil storm clouds above them arrived at Modi'im's city limits. The light rays of the morning sun were blocked out and a vast shadow overcame and covered the little valley village of Modi'im.

Commander Hippokrates signaled for the cavalry to slow their horses from a fast trot to a walk as they entered the city limits of the little valley village of Modi'im. He could hear the bleating of the large goat herds on the southern hills and his senses were filled with the effervescent odor from the intoxicating wine vats of the vast perfectly rowed vineyards. Immediately he was overcome with an unquenchable thirst for fine wine to sooth his parched throat. However, he must first attend to the important business at hand and find this man called Matityahu Maccabim *Kohen*, Priest, of Modi'im. Sergeant Lycus began questioning every traveler passing by and each villager gawking at them inquiring of them the whereabouts of one Matityahu Maccabim.

Finally, Commander Hippokrates raised his hand to stop the cavalry in front of the tin maker's shop. The middle aged man was busy hammering out a piece of tin into a wine goblet. He refused to stop his work and look up so Sergeant Lycus barked, "Peasant, we are looking for Matityahu Maccabim. Where is he?" The tin maker stopped his hammering and yelled, "Ya'aqob (Jacob)! Ya'aqob! Come here boy!" Around the corner of the shop ran a skinny little seven-year-old sandy-haired boy whose curls seemed to dance wildly upon the top of his head. He grinned from ear to ear as his pearl white teeth gleamed with joy shining from his olive brown face. When he saw the Commander and the cavalry his eyes got as big as two silver tetradrachm coins. "*Ken ab,* yes father," respectfully responded Ya'aqob, "here I am." The tin maker still did not look up from his work but instead extended his robed arm and pointed his finger down the highway to the west and said, "Ya'aqob take these men to *Kohen*, Priest, Matityahu at the dwelling next to the synagogue. Now *yalak,* walk." Ya'aqob quickly replied, "*Ken ab,* yes father."

The little olive-brown bare feet of Ya'aqob beat up and down on the dusty highway in a semi-running gate grinning ear-to-ear as he led Commander Hippokrates and his squadron to the residence of the *koen,* priest. The distance was only about one hundred and fifty yards but to this excited little seven year-old it was like being on a great adventure to a far away land. When they had reached their destination, Ya'aqob stopped in front of the house and pointed to the door and said, "Here." Then Sergeant Lycus snarled, "Good little gnat. Now get out of here before I swat you and let my horse stomp you into the ground!" Ya'aqob quickly obeyed and took off running back to the tin makers shop as fast as he could and did not even look back.

The whole squadron dismounted and stood by their horses as Sergeant Lycus held Hercules by the reigns for Commander Hippokrates who had gone to the wooden door and began beating on it with the butt end of his saddle crop. It only took a brief moment when the wooden door swung open with the figure of an aged man with a long grey beard standing in the open doorway. Commander Hippokrates puffed out his chest and held his head high, "We are looking for Matityahu Maccabim." Matityahu slowly gazed into the commander's eyes and said, "And just what are your intentions with this one Matityahu Maccabim?" At that moment his five sons put their hands on their daggers hidden behind their backs.

The dark storm clouds above began to rumble as the two evil hideous beasts gnawed at and pounded on the barriers of the clouds that restrained them from attacking this Hebrew family. Commander Hippokrates quickly and nervously glanced up at the thunderous clouds and then quipped, "That old man, would be the business between me and Matityahu. Now tell me where he is before I must teach you a lesson of respect." Once again the dark storm clouds rumbled with evil. Matityahu slowly lifted his hand to his grey beard, stroked it a few times and smiled with a reply, "Good sir, respect is something that you must earn and not be commanded." Then the clouds released a loud clap of thunder as the hyena sank its long sharp blood-stained teeth into the barrier and the massive gorilla threw all his weight into his clinched fists pounding on the barrier seeking to gain release to satisfy their craving for death and destruction. The sons of Matityahu tightened their fingers around their hidden daggers and the cavalry dropped the reigns of the horses and seized their spears along with their shields and got into attack formation.

Matityahu stared into the cold eyes of Commander Hippokrates and continued, "Sir, since I am Matityahu Maccabim, I am a man of great respect and as the village *kohen*, priest, I want to be hospitable. I am at your humble service. What can I do for you commander?" The thick tension in the air between the commander and the *kohen*, priest lessened at that moment a bit and the sons of Matityahu relaxed the grip on their hidden daggers slightly even though the soldiers remained on alert.

Commander Hippokrates stammered, "My apologies *Kohen* Matityahu of Modi'im. I have heard many fine things about you in Yruwshalaim. The dark storm clouds seem to be looming overhead so I must make our business brief. Our great king, Antiochus IV Epiphanes has left me in charge of law and order in the great city of Yruwshalaim. He only wishes, which is also my command, that all the people of his territories become one. In doing so they must all follow one law, which are his laws. This is where I need your help. As a man of deep respect in this territory and the great city of Yruwshalaim your persuasion in certain matters would be of great benefit to our king. I will see to it that you and your sons are well rewarded for your efforts in these certain matters of following his laws. Not only will you be considered a friend of the king but you and your children will receive large sums of silver, gold, houses, fine clothing and many more rewards. Can I count on your assistance? Choosing not to be a friend of the king can bring about serious and immediate consequences. I need an answer, now."

Kohen Matityahu lowered his eye contact a bit and slowly began stroking his beard as if in deep thought muttering one phrase over and over and over...*friend of the king....hmmm, friend of the king....* Thunder once again roared overhead as the thick dark clouds began to stir. The horses grew nervous so each soldier once again grabbed their reigns while Lycus held his horse and also old Hercules, the commander's black stallion. Then Matityahu wrung his hands together for what seemed to be an eternity but in reality was only for a minute. Next, he slapped his hands together and extended his arm towards Commander Hippokrates to embrace forearms as sealing an agreement.

At that instant, the hideous hyena and massive gorilla burst through the cloud barriers, extended their black wings and dove towards Matityahu and his sons. Evil was about to triumph and the evil beasts wanted blood on their wagging tongues. The hyena's mouth was open bearing all its sharp teeth as its hideous, eerie and bone-chilling laugh sent the dark clouds rolling. The gorilla fixed its glowing red eyes on the *kohen*, priest and opened its massive hands to grasp firmly the throat of Matityahu. They frantically beat their wings up and down to gain momentum in the attack of their unsuspecting victims. Thunder roared and it shook the earth as the beating of the hideous monsters wings beat frantically in the air.

Matityahu and Commander Hippokrates grasped forearms and Matityahu said, "*Ken*, yes and....." At this pause Matityahu looked fully into the cold eyes of Commander Hippokrates and smiled through his full gray beard. Hyena and Gorilla extended their long sharp claws and fingernails and was nearly about to make contact with their victims when out of nowhere a great light shone between them and the Hebrew men. The light was so bright it blinded them and a mighty force of wind caused them to collide into each other with a great thud. The impact sent both beasts tumbling out of control through the air spinning head over heels. Hyena tried to get its black body under control but caught the tip of the rotating sword just under its protruding ribcage. This sent the creature howling in immense pain and it beat a hasty retreat back to Satan's cauldron. However, the Gorilla had gained its balance and was just ready to close its massive hands around the tender neck of the aged *kohen*, priest, when the handle of the rotating sword smacked it upside its big protruding forehead. Dazed and oozing a thick red stream from the deep laceration now in the middle of its forehead, all it could manage was a half-hearted roar as it pounded its massive chest with one fist and the other placed over the deep cut on its forehead. The rapid rotating sword whirled and sang in the air like a propeller engine preparing for takeoff. The massive beast stood erect on its massive tree trunk legs as if to challenge the rotating sword again, but had to use both hands to cover its ears from the whir of the rotating blade. Then the hideous beast turned and bid a hasty retreat back to the pits of hell where it came from, no longer wanting to challenge the undefeatable power of Yahuah Yahusha.

A single sunbeam sliced through the thick dark storm clouds and as they quickly parted and the mid-day sun shone down upon the village town of Modi'im. Then Matityahu Maccabim finished his sentence,"......and *lo*, no!" Commander Hippokrates released his grip and puzzled said, "Just what is that supposed to mean?" Matityahu replied with a broadening smile, "*Ken*, yes, I am curious and want to learn more about this notion of following one law, the law of the king that will make me his friend and *lo*, no, I will not give you my final answer today. My sons and I will travel to the great city of Yruwshalaim tomorrow to see firsthand what persuasion of my respect is needed to assist the king."

Commander Hippokrates grabbed the reigns of Hercules from Lycus and the entire cavalry mounted their horses at the command of "Mount up!" As they headed east on the dusty highway to exit the village town of Modi'im Sergeant Lycus said to Commander Hippokrates, "Zeus has smiled upon you today, commander." Meanwhile, back at the residence of Matityahu his sons exclaimed, "*Ab*, father, what have you done? Have you conspired with the enemy?" The aged *kohen*, softly replied, "My sons, you just witnessed my foot being placed upon the head of a great and dangerous snake. Mark my words, by this time tomorrow he will find his own lying forked-tongue being pierced by the teeth of his own mouth. May Yahuah grant us a blessing of a good night's rest because tomorrow will be a very long and exhausting day."

4

Early the next morning as a group of grey and white colored turtledoves were perched above the Yeshenah Gate cooing as if to welcome the travels approaching the great city of Yruwshalaim, Matityahu and his five sons all riding on donkeys approached the tall and thick woodenplanked western gate. Since the light of dawn had shown brightly for some time now, the massive wooden gates hung open on their hinges. However, two soldiers with long sharp spears stood in the opening questioning each and every traveler coming in and going out of the great city.

The six men from the village of Modi'im approached the opening and the gruff guard lowered his spear and said, "Halt there! This city has enough donkeys on its streets we don't need a dozen more! Turn around and go back home dung heaps!" Now both guards were laughing at the six Hebrew men on their donkeys. Matityahu said, "Gentlemen, we have business here in the city with Commander Hippokrates. Please let us pass." The gruff soldier snarled, "Commander Hippokrates does not do business with any swine unless it has been sacrificed upon the altar of Zeus and is finely roasted. Oh, maybe you came to be roasted to our great god." Once again clamorous laughter broke out among the two guards. However, the laughter quickly ceased as Yhuwdah (Judas) quipped, "Silence your tongue soldier or I will have to remove it from your mouth! You are speaking dishonorably to the *kohen*, priest, of the village of Modi'im." The gruff solider responded, "Whoa, pardon me. If

Hebrew people are stinking swine, than I should pay my respects to the boss hog!" The five sons jumped off the backs of their donkeys and reached for their daggers when three mounted patrol arrived to see what all the commotion was about.

"What kind of disturbance is going on here!" commanded Sergeant Lycus. The gruff guard saluted and cowering said to his superior, "These Hebrew swine are demanding to meet with Commander Hippokrates and I am politely trying to tell them to go back home as the Commander is very busy today." "You nit-wit. By whose authority have you been appointed the Commander's private Master of Audiences? Now step aside and let me speak to them," scowled Sergeant Lycus. As the Sergeant moved his horse forward, he recognized the six Hebrew men and apologetically said, "*Kohen* Maccabim, welcome to this great city. I will personally escort you and your sons directly to the Temple." Sergeant Lycus pivoted his steed on it haunches and knocked to the ground the gruff guard. The guard quickly rolled out of the way before he got stepped on by the six donkeys entering the gate, coughing and gagging from eating and breathing the dust of the animals as they passed him by.

They arrived at the beautiful Temple that had been rebuilt after the Hebrew captivity in Babylon. Sergeant Lycus commanded Matityahu and his sons to wait outside because Commander Hippokrates wanted to finish his business with them first before they would be allowed to go inside to worship. The three mounted patrol galloped away to inform the Commander that his guests had arrived. The morning sun was growing hot and after half an hour wait Commander Hippokrates arrived with great pomp. Commander Hippokrates got out of his litter carrier which had been carried by eight large black-skinned Nubean eunuchs who were naked except for their loincloths. Their huge black bodies shone in the morning light as perspiration moistened their bodies. They stood at attention by the litter carrier as Hippokrates approached the six Hebrew men saying, "Ahhhh, respected *Kohen,* priest, Matityahu. Glad you could make it this morning. I have summoned your High Priest, Azaryah to join us immediately in order for us to complete our important business. I anxiously await your decision to use your persuasion to help these people to carry out the new law of the land as commanded by his Excellency Antiochus IV Epiphanes. As a matter of fact, here comes Azaryah now down the street. Let's go inside where it is cooler instead of standing out here sweating in the hot sun."

Just as the golden doors of the Temple were closed, Hippokrates nodded in the direction of Azaryah and said, "Azaryah, you are the High Priest of this Temple yet you refuse to embrace the new worship laws of our king. Matityahu Maccabim, the *kohen* of the village of Modi'im has agreed to embrace and encourage obedience to the laws of our king. If you continue to refuse to embrace these changes and obey just as respected Matityahu has done, then with the authority vested in me by his Excellency Antiochus IV Epiphanes I will dismiss you and fill your position with someone who will represent true worship in this city and throughout the king's kingdom." At that moment, *HaGadowl Kohen* Azaryah's startled eyes met with the aged eyes of Matityahu's in total bewilderment. Thoughts of betrayal ran rampant in Azaryah's mind…*Was this the wise council that Matityahu was going to deliver to me? I wonder what was his price of treason?* His thoughts were interrupted by the sound of Matityahu's voice, "Commander Hippokrates, I must see the altar of worship." "Oh yes, by all means. You're in a hurry to get started on the job, eh? Your vast reward of riches and honor will begin today. I am pleased that you have come to your senses and accepted my proposition," he said with an egotistical smile. Sharp dagger looks went from the eyes of Azaryah to Matityahu as he thought *I knew he sold out. I am doomed!*

When the golden oak-leaf inner doors of the Holy Place opened, Matityahu almost fell down in astonishment and disgust as he saw the blood spattered walls, the adulterous image of the dragon dedicated to Zeus and a pagan Gentile officer standing in the Most Sacred Place where the Sacred Box between two large Cherubim had once stood. A couple of steps inside with Azaryah close on his heels, Matityahu spun around and faced Commander Hippokrates. Azaryah noted that the demeanor of Matityahu was no longer playing out a charade but had outfoxed the 'old fox' Hippokrates. Even the veins in the neck of Matityahu were shaking and inflamed with zeal. Azaryah, *HaGadowl Kohen,* the High Priest, raised his hands towards Yahuah Yahusha in praise.

Now the aged *kohen,* priest, was burning with righteous anger and he screamed at the Commander, "Contrary to your own self-delusion, I have not given you my final answer until this very moment! That answer is *Lo!* No! Even though all the nations under the king's dominion obey him and everyone falls away from the religion of their fathers and give consent to his commands, yet I and my five sons and our families will walk in the covenant of our fathers with Yahuah. May it never be that we should forsake His laws and His ordinances! We will not listen to the king's words or walk away from our faith of Yahuah, either to the right hand or to the left. Now, this conversation with you is *gamar,* ended. You are *gowy,* Gentile, and contaminate this Holy Place like *galal,* dung balls. *Yalak! Yalak!* Walk away and get out of here!"

Yhuwdah (Judas) and Yowchanan (John) the sons of Matityahu grabbed the doors and slammed them shut dividing the two opposing parties. On the inside of the Holy Place and the Most Holy Place was *HaGadowl Kohen* Azaryah, *Kohen* Matityahu Maccabim, his five faithful sons, and two wide-eyed spectators that were previously unseen. On the outside was a very irate Commander with his soldiers. A loud thud and a clink could be heard from the outside as the helmet of the Commander was hurled at the closed doors. Hippokrates yelled, "Guards, bar these doors and don't let anyone out or escape. If they are not all accounted for when I return you shall forfeit your lives!"

Matityahu ran to the front of the Most Sacred Place where a Helene (Greek) officer was ordering a Hebrew man to slaughter a pig on the altar of Zeus. Just as the Hebrew was ready to slit the throat of the pig Matityahu grabbed the hand of the Hebrew that held the sacrificial knife. Matityahu yelled, "*Lo!*, no, my brother." The Hebrew struggled with Matityahu and argued, "Leave me alone, *kohen*, priest. I need to sacrifice to my god." Then Matityahu said, "Then die with your god but you will not *kane*, bend the knee, to Zeus!" Matityahu quickly overpowered the Hebrew man and guided the sacrificial knife deep under the Hebrew man's rib cage and the man fell to the floor in a heap. The Helene (Greek) officer lunged at Matityahu and Matityahu caught the officer in the throat with a dagger that had been well hidden in his front belt beneath his *kohen*, priest, robe.

Azaryah thinking quickly said, "Quick, you and your sons must escape through this secret chamber. Then you must go out the Huldah Gates on the south side of the Royal Porch into the Tyropoeon Valley located in the Lower City. You must move very swiftly going to the Pool Siloam and there as *kohen*, priest, you will recognize the priestly secret of the Tunnel of Hezekiah. There you can vanish in the hills south of the Mount of Olives and the town of Bethany. *Shalom* my brothers, *Shalom*." Then Azaryah went to the doors as a diversion and beat on them yelling, "Guards, a travesty. Guards, Guards! Open the doors!"

Matityahu and his five sons vanished through the secret chamber of the Holy of Holies which led to the Huldah Gates on the south side of the Royal Porch. The gates were not guarded since the soldiers had gone to the Temple gate Beautiful to help with all the commotion. They swiftly went out the Huldah Gates and then began shouting in the Lower City with a loud voice, "Whoever is zealous of the law of Yahuah and maintains His covenant, hurry and come follow us." The revolt had begun with about forty men escaping into the wilderness of the hills east of the great city of Yruwshalaim. As the little band of forty Hebrew men made their way up the steep craggy clefts of the hills east of the great city, they could see moving torches as if they were yellow fireflies flittering all about and could hear a great commotion. However, this little band moved silently concentrating on their footing in the darkness of the shadows of the great hills. After two hours of picking their way carefully through the sharp craggy clefts, they reached their *m'lunah*, place to sleep. Matityahu looked out over the top of the rocks that were providing their secret cover as a hideout, yet the moon was not providing enough light to see if this was a good place to keep out of the reach of the Helene (Greek) soldiers. It would just have to wait until the morning light. Now was the time to rest and tomorrow to make plans.

Matityahu was suddenly awakened in the pre-dawn light by the screeching of a hawk hovering and gliding effortlessly on the currents of air looking for a mouse or a small rabbit as a breakfast morsel. His aged bones felt stiff after such a long night and sleeping on the hard and cold rocks. As his lungs inhaled the brisk air of the coolness of the morning, reality of the previous day's events began to sink in. First on the list was that they had to warn their families in Modi'im and Yruwshalaim and get them safely to the hideout before the sunrise of the next day. Then there was the matter of the provision of food, clothing, weapons and shelter because no fires could be built as that would give their location away to the Helene (Greek) soldiers below.

During the next twelve months the little band of forty Hebrew men grew to about three-hundred men with their families. They avenged the massacres by the Helenes (Greeks) that took place in the village of Modi'im, which killed one-thousand men, women and children on the Sabbath as the Helene (Greek) soldiers searched for those involved in what historians would later call the "Maccabees Revolt" led by one Matityahu Maccabim.

Now a year later in 166 B.C. his aged body was giving out and he was about to die. He called his five sons close to him and he said, "Now my sons be zealous for the Law of Yahuah and give your lives for the covenant of your fathers with Yahuah. Call to remembrance what acts our fathers did in their time and so shall you receive great honor and an everlasting name. Always remember that all who put their trust in Him shall not be overcome. Do not fear then the words of sinful man because for his glory will be dung and worms."

"Therefore, my sons, be valiant and show yourselves men on behalf of the Law of Yahuah for by it you shall obtain glory. Behold, I know your brother Shim'one (Simon) is a man of great counsel, give your ears unto him always and he will be a father to you. As for Yhuwdah (Judas) Maccabim he has been mighty and strong, even from his youth up. Let him be your captain and fight the battle of the people. Take also unto you all those that observe the Law of Yahuah and avenge the wrong of your people." Then with his last breath, Matityahu Maccabim blessed his sons and was gathered to his fathers. He died at the age of one-hundred and twenty years old and his sons buried him in the sepulchers of the village of Modi'im. The courage of one aged *kohen*, priest, from the little valley village of Modi'm would change history forever, ushering in the coming of the promised Messiah predicted by the prophets of long ago, even unto *Olam Haba*, the world to come.

5

Near the end of the year 166 B.C., following the death of Matityahu, Yhuwdah (Judas) Maccabim the third son of Matityahu became the captain and *HaGadowl Kohen,* High Priest, of the revolt against the abomination set contrary to the Law of Yahuah. All of his brothers helped him and so did all that followed his father. They all were glad to follow Yhuwdah as captain and willingly fought the battle of Yisra'Yah (Israel). Yhuwdah (Judas) brought great honor to his people and was a mighty *gammed*, warrior for Yahuah with a brilliant military mind. He and his army engaged in many battles and protected the loyal Hebrews with his sword. His actions were like a mighty lion and like a young lion roaring loudly for his prey. He pursued the wicked and sought them out and set on fire those who persecuted his people, the Hebrews. Therefore, the wicked shrunk and trembled with great fear of his name and all the workers of iniquity were troubled because salvation, *Yahusha*, prospered in his hand. He grieved many kings as he went through the cities of the territory of Yhuwdah (Judah known as Judea by the Greeks and Romans) destroying the ungodly out of them and turning away the wrath of Yahuah from Yisra'Yah (Israel). His name became renowned throughout all the corners of the earth and he was nicknamed 'The Hebrew Hammer'.

His bothers also were affectionately known by their nicknames. Yowchanan (John) the oldest was known as Caddis meaning 'My Fortune' and Shim'own (Simon) the second son was known as Thassi meaning 'The Zealous'. El'azar (Eliezer) the fourth son was known as Avaran meaning 'The Piercer' because he was an expert with the spear and finally the fifth and youngest son Yownathan (Jonathan) was known as Apphus meaning 'The Diplomat'. All were valiant *gammedim*, warriors, and fought for His Law and Commandments with intense dedication and savage wrath against His enemies. Even though they fought great battles and performed heroic feats, it was not their military prowess and bravery that made them the most famous. Their love and dedication to Yahuah Yahusha was first to fall from the lips of those who gave them accolades.

In the spring of 165 B.C. Yhuwdah Maccabim was mindful of the superiority of the Helene (Greek) military forces so his strategy was to avoid any engagement with their regular army and resorted to guerilla warfare in order to give the Hellenes (Greeks) the feeling of insecurity through ambushes and clever traps. Not only did this bring fear among small detachments of Helene (Greek) soldiers but created enthusiasm among the Hebrew men who left their homes in throngs to join this new captain of Yahuah Yahusha. After a string of small victories by the Hebrew army, Apollonius the governor and general of Samaria took a small Assyrian force of nine-hundred men to come against Yhuwdah and his Hebrew army at the battle of Nahal el-Haramiah (Wadi Haramia). The Assyrian general was killed by Yhuwdah and he took his sword which he used until his own death as a symbol of vengeance. This victory led to many more recruits who flocked to the Hebrew camp to join the cause to defend the Law and Commandments of Yahuah Yahusha.

In the early fall of 165 B.C. Antiochus IV Epiphanes, the Helen (Greek) king of Syria left to Parthia (Persia, modern Iran) to gather tributes from countries on the way and to amass a large sum of money to refill his treasuries which had been depleted by dissension and a plague. He put Viceroy Lysias, a member of the royal bloodline and a nobleman, in charge to squelch the Hebrew revolt in Yhuwdah (Judea). Therefore, Lysias commanded his generals Seron, Nicanor and Gorgias to take their armies and to totally crush the Maccabim army of the Hebrews. When the smaller and outnumbered army of Yhuwdah (Judas) saw the much larger and well equipped army of the Helene (Greek) generals, they cried out, "How shall we be able, being so few, to fight against such a great multitude who are so strong? We are faint from marching and fasting all day long"

Yhuwdah calmly said in a loud confident voice, "Hebrew brothers be still and listen to me! It is not such a hard matter for so many to be given into the hands of so few. With Yahuah in Heaven it doesn't matter whether our enemies are a great multitude or a small company. He can deliver either one into our hands for a victory. You see, they come against us in great pride and iniquity to destroy us, our wives and our children, but we fight for our lives and for the Law and Commandments of Yahuah. The victory of the battle does not come from the strength of a great multitude but from the power of Heaven. Yahuah Himself will overthrow them in front of our face and as for you, do not fear!"

When he had finished speaking, the Hebrew army gave a great shout and sprang upon the Helene (Greek) multitude in a surprise attack. By a forced night march, Yhuwdah had succeeded in eluding Gorgias and his army as they had intended to attack and destroy the Hebrew forces in their camp with his cavalry. At the same time, Nicanor and his army was helping Gorgias searching for Yhuwdah in the mountains. This left only Seron to face the Hebrew army on the battlefield near Beyth-Horon. Then the Hebrew army proceeded to pound the armies of Nicanor and Gorgias in the Battle of Emmaus five miles northwest of the great city of Yruwshalaim. Since the great multitude of the Helenes (Greeks) was split up, the three armies did not have any alternative but to withdraw all the way to the sea coast of the Great Mediterranean Sea. However, only one-hundred Helene (Greek) soldiers survived with eight-hundred men from their three armies and General Seron were left dead on the two battlefields.

Then Antiochus IV Epiphanes heard the news of this great defeat and was filled with indignation that the Hebrew army was encamped at Emmaus only five miles northwest of Yruwshalaim. So in the late fall of 165 B.C. he sent word from Parthia (Persia/modern Iran) to Viceroy Lysias with instructions to gather half of all his forces and rout the Hebrew revolt once and for all. He also sent word to have his son, Antiochus V, to rule Syria and its western territories until he returned again to Antioch. Lysias chose Ptolemy the son of Dorymenes as a general to replace Seron and also generals Gorgias and Nicanor, close friends of the king, to lead the attack from the north. While the three generals would be attacking from north, he would take his army and gather in Idumea (Edom) to attack from the south of the city of Yruwshalaim, with Commander Hippokrates controlling the garrison and the great city, leaving no escape of a retreat for the rag-tag army of "The Hebrew Hammer", Yhuwdah Maccabim.

The rag-tag army of Yhuwdah Maccabim and his brothers now numbered three-thousand *gammedim,* warriors, but only about half of them had any swords or armor. The rest were armed with wooden pitch-forks, hammers, clubs and a few bows. Their Helene (Greek) enemies on the other hand were a great and vast multitude. In the spring of 164 B.C. the northern Helene (Greek) army arrived ten miles north of the village of Emmaus, the camp of the Hebrew army. On the right flank was General Nicanor with twenty-thousand foot soldiers and a three-thousand horse cavalry. In the center and the commander of the invasion was Gorgias with five-thousand elite foot soldiers, one-thousand of the finest cavalry of horses and riders and in front of them were one-hundred elephants with skilled bowmen. The left flank was protected by General Ptolemy with fifteen-thousand foot soldiers bearing spears and swords along with a three-thousand horse cavalry. The total army invading the village of Emmaus from the north was forty-thousand foot soldiers, seven-thousand horses and one-hundred elephants.

On the south of the city of Yruwshalaim from the territory of Idumea, the land of the Edomiy, Lysias was marching with a massive army of sixty-thousand foot soldiers, five-thousand cavalry horses and riders and two-hundred elephants with bowmen. This massive Helene (Greek) army totaled one-hundred thousand foot soldiers, a cavalry of twelve-thousand horses and riders and three-hundred elephants carrying skilled bowmen. Yes, the Hebrew army only numbered fifteen hundred armed *gammedim,* warriors and another fifteen hundred unarmed men with three-hundred *showphars,* curved ram horn trumpets, but they had the mighty hand of protection of the undefeatable Yahuah Yahusha. Yhuwdah would attack the city of Yruwshalaim and Commander Hippokrates with one-hundred men, while Yowchanan (John) and Yonathan (Jonathan) would defend the north with twelve-hundred men and Shim'one (Simon) and El'azar (Eliezer) would defend the south with seventeen-hundred men. They would stay tightly bunched and protect each other in an arching formation.

It was supposed to be a holy Sabbath as it was the 14th day of the month of Abib also called Nisan. Instead of engaging in a war, the Hebrew *gammedim,* warriors should have been celebrating *Pecach,* Passover. The festival comemerating when Mosheh (Moses) led the Hebrews out of Egypt to this Promise Land. However, Yhuwdah signaled and the three-hundred *showphars,* curved ram horn trumpets, sounded the long continuous blast of war. Then the great battle for the spiritual freedom of Yahuah Yahusha's people in His land began. Even the devout Hebrew people remaining in the great city of Yruwshalaim began an uprising when they heard the deafening sound of the trumpets against the Grecian-Jews and the Helene (Greek) Commander Hippokrates confining him and his soldiers to the garrison.

Within the first hour of fighting, Lysias had lost five-thousand foot soldiers on the battlefield. The fierce battle raged on for eight long new moons (months). Yhuwdah's Hebrew rag-tag army only numbered one-thousand brave men leaving two-thousand dead on the battlefield. They were very tired and weary but refused to give up. They continually prayed for renewed strength with each swing of the sword or thrust of the spear. Yahuah Yahusha answered as the total of the northern and southern Helene (Greek) army currently only numbered five thousand foot soldiers and two-hundred cavalry. Lysias and his three military generals had lost ninety-five thousand dead or deserted foot soldiers, eleven-thousand eight-hundred cavalry horses that had been run off or captured and all three-hundred elephants had been scattered from the battlefield. Over the past eight months of heavy fighting the Hebrew army had worked its way within a quarter of a mile from the walls of the great city of Yruwshalaim.

As it grew dark on the 25th day of the month of Kislev in 164 B.C. (December 14th, 164 B.C.) something surprising happened that gave strength to the outnumbered Hebrew army just outside the city walls. The houses in the great city of Yruwshalaim were lit with torches and even the golden Mnowrah Chandelier lamp stand, which had been replaced, was lit in the Temple with the last container of oil that had been sealed by the *HaGadowl Koen*, High Priest,

Azaryah. The container of oil would only last one night and it would take eight days to make more oil according to the Law of Mosheh (Moses) in the statutes of temple worship but maybe it would give hope to the brave *gammedim*, warriors for at least one night. Word spread quickly throughout the ranks of the Hebrew army that the golden Mnowrah Chandelier had been lit symbolizing the presence of Yahuah Yahusha. It was in reference of the burning bush when Mosheh (Moses) was instructed to lead the people of Yahuah Yahusha out of slavery in the land of Mitsrayim (Egypt) to the Promise Land that was conquered by Yhowshuwa (Joshua) and the twelve tribes in 1398 B.C. Now, twelve-hundred and thirty-four years later, a group of brave Hebrew men were fighting once again for the freedom to practice the Law and Commandments of Yahuah Yahusha.

The *gammedim*, warriors, of Yahuah Yahusha commanded by Yhuwdah (Judas) Maccabim did gain courage from the light of the city and began to fight more fiercely throughout the next day. Then on the second night to the surprise of the *kohen*, priest, a miraculous thing was witnessed. The perfumed olive oil reserve of the Mnowrah Chandelier lamp stand was not depleted and the Mnowrah Chandelier lamp stand was burning brightly. News of this miracle quickly spread throughout the great city of Yruwshalaim and every house created burning lights of some sort. This miracle occurred six more nights with the Mnowrah Chandelier lamp stand burning brightly and the oil reserve not going dry, giving the Hebrew men great hope. Then on the eight night just after sunset, Yhuwdah and his Hebrew army totally crushed the once massive Helene (Greek) army sending the remaining soldiers into fast retreat. Yhuwdah and the one-thousand remaining *gammedim*, warriors, of Yahuah Yahusha entered the gates of Yruwshalaim on the 3rd day of the month of Tevet (December 21st, 164 B.C.) and marched straight to the Temple. Azaryah the

HaGadowl Kohen, High Priest, of Yruwshalaim greeted Yhuwdah Maccabim the *HaGadowl Kohen*, High Priest, of the Hebrew people with open arms and a holy kiss on both cheeks and retold the story of the miracle of perfumed olive oil and the never-ending light from the golden Mnowrah Chandelier lamp stand. Yhuwdah and Azaryah tore down the figure of the dragon dedicated to Zeus and had the Temple cleaned.

After a week's rest Yhuwdah summoned all the people of the city of Yruwshalaim and its surrounding villages to the Temple for a rededication. He said in a loud voice from the top steps of the Temple, "I remember a song by our Father David which his son Shlomoh (Solomon) used when he dedicated the first house of Yahuah, number thirty of the book Thillahyim (Psalms)." Then *Kohen* Yhuwdah raised both his arms and looked towards the heavens and sang, "I will raise you high oh Yahuah because You have delivered me and have not let my hating adversaries be gleeful over me. Oh Yahuah, my Yah, I have cried for help to You and You have mended and cured me. Oh Yahuah You have ascended up from Sh'owl, the world of the dead, my vitality of breath. You have kept me alive from descending down into the Pit Hole. Celebrate in song and music accompanied by voice and the striking of the fingers on the strings of musical instruments to Yahuah, kind saints. Extend the hands in worship for the memory of His sacredness. Because in a very short space of time, in the wink of an eye is His anger from His rapid breathing nostrils. Life is His delight. At dusk weeping that drips may stay overnight but in the morning at dawn the break of day is a shout of acclamation"

"I will say in my security, I will not waver, slip, shake or fall to the vanishing point of eternity. Oh Yahuah in Your delight You made to stand my strong mountain. You kept secret Your face and I trembled inwardly with anxiety. To You oh Yahuah I will call out and to my Sovereign I will lift supplication prayers. What gain is there for my blood descending down to the Pit Hole? Will the powdered gray clay dust extend its hands in worship to You? Will it announce by word of mouth the stability of Your truth? Hear intelligently oh Yahuah and stoop in kindness and favor to me. Oh Yahuah exist as protection and aid to me. You have turned about my lamentation into round dancing for me. You have lowered my course mesh cloth used for grain bags that I have put on for mourning and have belted me with religious glee. Therefore, my weighty splendor will celebrate in song and music accompanied by voices and the striking with fingers the strings of musical instruments and will not be silent. Oh Yahuah, my Yah to the vanishing point of eternity I will extend my hands in worship."

Then Yhuwdah Maccabim lowered his arms and looked at the crowd and commanded, "The Temple of Yahuah has been rededicated to Him today. Forever, it will be an everlasting statute that on the 25th of Kislev of each year this day forward will be a celebration for eight consecutive days the Feast of Dedication called *Chanukah*, Hanukkah. It will also be known as the Festival of Lights and a special golden Mnowrah Chandelier lamp stand will be lit. It will have nine lights with one raised in the center and four lower lights on the right of the raised light and four lower lights on the left of the raised light. The raised center light shall be called the *shamash*, meaning attendant because Yahuah Yahusha was present with His light of hope and attended to our needs. On the first night, you shall first light the *shamash*, the center light attendant. Then you shall light the light which is on the far right with the *shamach*, attendant. Each night you shall first light the *shamach*, attendant, and using it you shall add one more light starting at the right and ending on the left until all eight lower lights are lit on the eighth day. This shall be done in remembrance to all generations of the great victory that Yahuah has provided for us and the story of the miracle of the perfumed olive oil which was never depleted providing a light of hope in our struggles."

Then Yhuwdah (Judas) took over the garrison in the city of Yruwshalaim as his military command center and executed Commander Hippokrates and Sergeant Lycus along with many of the loyal Helene (Greek) soldiers. Other regions of the territory of Yhuwdah (Judea) cried out for help from 'The Hebrew Hammer.' The regions of Gilead, Transjordan and Galilee were all under attack by the retreating armies of the Helene (Greek) kingdom of King Antiochus IV Epiphanes. Maybe the 'miracle of light', Hanukkah, should be shared elsewhere and throughout time until eternity.

6

The dark demonic skies that loomed over the evil cauldron of Satan were filled with eerie screams and howling as the wounded and defeated forces of darkness returned to their wicked lair from doing spiritual battle over the city of Yruwshalaim. The vast number of pitch black gargoyles limped through the air with battered wings and deep lacerations as a thick dark ooze with the stench of death seeped from their wounds. Satan's minions once again failed to carry out their master's command to destroy worship and fellowship to Yahuah Yahusha. Even his great puppet, king Antiochus IV Epiphanes of Helene (Greek) rule died in Parthia (Persia, modern Iran) within a few days of the defeat and fall of the great city of Yruwshalaim back in the control of the Hebrew people. The constant taste of defeat enraged the dark lord of wickedness. His army that tried to do his bidding were met back home with searing flames of fire and the chocking odor of burning sulfur and brimstone. What did he have to do to defeat this Great Light that blinded his ranks of evil conspiracies and then wounded them with a Rotating Sword that sang with a high pitch roar? *Someday the worship of all mankind will belong to me and only me!*, Satan thought. Maybe the new year of 163 B.C. will be kinder to his self-serving prideful mission. However, now at this moment of time he had to regroup and conspire another plan of treachery and wickedness against mankind.

Yhuwdah (Judas) listened to the desperate pleas of the territories of Gilead, Transjordan and Galilee. He sent Shim'own (Simon) his brother with an army of three-thousand *gammedim*, warriors, to the territory of Galilee. His brothers, Yowchanan (John) and El'azar (Eliezer) he sent to the territory of the Transjordan with five-thousand *gammedim*, warriors. To the territory of Gilead, he himself and his brother Yownathan (Jonathan) marched an army of eight-thousand *gammedim*, warriors. After, six months of marching and doing battle, all three armies returned at mid-summer of 163 B.C. back to the great city of Yruwshalaim victorious after only losing a total of two-thousand brave men. Shim'own (Simon) routed Ptolemee and his raiding bands killing three-thousand men loyal to the Helene (Greek) throne. Yowchanan (John) and El'azar (Eliezer) killed General Nicanor along with four-thousand men fighting for Helene (Greek) oppression upon the Hebrew people. Yhuwdah (Judas) and Yownathan (Jonathan) demolished Georias and killed eight-thousand men before the general took his wounded and depleted army back to Syria. Generals Ptolemee and Georias were met in Antioch with great indignation by Viceroy Lysias and the new king Antiochus V Eupator. Lysias exclaimed, "Ptolemee you have failed twice now and you, Georias you have miserably been defeated three times now!" The new king Antiochus V Eupator chimed in, "You may have been friends of my father but I will not tolerate failure. Today you will join him in the underworld of the dead"

In 162 B.C. Viceroy Lysias and crowned king Antiochus V Eupator gathered a great multitude to come up against Yishra'Yah (Israel) and Yhuwdah Maccabim. They gathered their Syrian army from all the other kingdoms and the Philistines, men from the isles of the seas, bands of murderous mercenaries hired by Syria, and the nation of Idumea (Edom) under the leadership of the tribal leader Herod Atticus. The Herod family got their name from the Aramaic word *herod*, meaning 'hero'. They spent many days in

Idumea (Edom) building engines of warfare but during a night raid Hebrew villagers from Beyth-sura came out and set them on fire and burned them to the ground. Thus the mighty Hellenistic (Grecian) army consisted of one-hundred thousand foot soldiers with spears, shields and swords, twenty-thousand cavalry horses and riders, and thirty-two elephants with bowmen. They drugged the elephants with the blood of grapes and mulberries to encourage them to go into battle. They divided the elephants among the armies appointing each great beast one-thousand men armed with coats of mail, helmets of bronze on their heads and five-hundred of the best cavalry horsemen. Upon the elephants were great towers of wood which covered every one of them with thirty-two bowmen with their Indian driver. When the bright mid-day sun shone upon the thousands of shields of gold and brass helmets they glistened like lamps of fire upon the white limestone hills and also filled the valley near the village of Beyth-zechariah located eight miles south of Beyth Lechem (Bethlehem) and eighteen miles south of the great city Yruwshalaim. Here the forces of good and evil would meet once again. Would Satan's forces conquer?

Yhuwdah (Judas) once again massed his forces including the *Chaciydim* (Hasidim), the pious Hebrew Rabbi's who went beyond enforcing the Law and Commandments. They had joined forces with his father Matityahu five years earlier when the revolt had first begun. They were among the first to leave the city of Yruwshalaim to join the band of rebels in the camp behind the rocky clefts. Now they stood beside Yhuwdah once again to repel the forces of spiritual slavery. Yhuwdah had an army of twenty-thousand Hebrew *gammedim*, warriors plus the prayers of faith to Yahuah Yahusha to turn back this great tide of Hellenism.

The war elephants and light infantry were at the helm of the attack with a heavy cavalry and chariots anchoring the flanks on the high ground. In the center rear marched the shock troops of heavy infantry in a phalanx formation, which was a rectangular mass military formation covered by shields and long heavy spears that took two hands to handle them. Yhuwdah did not defer to his usual guerilla tactics that had given him success in the past because he felt that they would expect a non-traditional defense. Therefore, Yhuwdah and his Hebrew *gammedim*, warriors used traditional military field tactics and fought the Helenes (Greeks) in their own fashion. This caused a temporary defeat and a quick withdrawal back to the hills to regroup.

The oncoming war elephants unnerved the troops of Yhuwdah as the Hebrews broke for the rear. Then El'azar Maccabim the second to the youngest brother of Yhuwdah, showed great courage to rally the troops perceiving that one of the elephants was decorated with a royal harness and was higher than all the rest, thinking that king Antiochus V Eupator was aboard. Therefore, he put himself in jeopardy to give the *gammedim*, warriors encouragement and ran courageously through the midst of the battle slaying foot soldiers on the right hand and of the left hand just as if he was parting the Red Sea. Then El'azar nicknamed "Avaran" meaning, the Piercer, crept under the great-war elephant and thrust a long spear into its soft belly and the elephant died immediately falling on top of El'azar, killing him. Yet, this act of bravery was not enough to rally the Hebrew forces, which collapsed under the heavy pressure of the Helene (Greek) phalanx. Yhuwdah and the Hebrew troops retreated back to the stronghold of the great city of Yruwshalaim where they inflicted heavy casualties upon the army of Antiochus V Eupator and Viceroy Lysias. The newly crowned king refused to suffer a defeat and decided to propose a peaceful settlement to Yhuwdah

(Judas). The terms of this settlement was based on the restoration of religious freedom, the permission for the Hebrews to live in accordance with their own laws, and the official return of the Temple to the Hebrew people. However, the *HaGadawl Kohen*, High Priest, had to be selected by the king with minor approval by the Hebrew political parties. The agreement was ratified and the king selected Alcimus Yakim, meaning in Hebrew "Established by Yahuah". He was a Hellenistic Hebrew from a line of *kohen*, priests, descent which pleased the political party of the *Chaciydim*, Hasidim. Then they mourned the death of El'azar Maccabim "The Piercer" in 162 B.C., the brother of Yhuwdah (Judas) and the fourth son of Matityahu Maccabim throughout the entire land of Yhuwdah.

Two years later, in 160 B.C. the black evil boiling cauldron of Satan began bellowing great puffs of thick black smoke. He had concocted the perfect potion of wickedness to bring death and destruction to the people loyal to Yahuah Yahusha. His strategy changed from using brute force by military conquest to one of gradual small deceptions spawned through a new and rising government. The changes and deceptions would be so small it would be like turning up the heat gradually on a frog in hot water on a stove. Before mankind knew what was happening they would be in boiling water and could not reverse the process of being cooked to death. Now the evil cauldron belched a constant rising of wicked smoke causing the demons to become anxious for their next assignment of demise. Then a legion of pitch black serpents with heads and long necks like anacondas, a mid-section like an elephant, the tails of scorpions and large black wings with a twenty foot span like a buzzard ascended up from the belching smoke of the evil caldron and headed towards Rome. The venom of these creatures incited betrayal, greed, murder and an unquenchable thirst for power. Their victims quickly would succumb to the great god called Mammon and Satan, its master would finally have his victory over mankind.

The Roman Senate decided in 160 B.C. to conquer Helene (Greek) civilizations because of their weak economy, yet seem to control unlimited resources of wealth and land. Roman counsel Ludius Mummius led the charge in the Senate while the Helene bred Senator Demetrius I Soter, son of Seleucus IV Philopator and nephew of the late king Antiochus IV Epiphanes defended the interests of Macedonia. Demetrius was largely outnumbered as the intention of the political parties of Rome was to be a world power not the tail of a wagging dog. Demetrius I Soter fled from Rome in defiance of the Roman Senate and headed straight to Antioch Syria. When arriving he found the king, his cousin, Antiochus V Eupator and Viceroy Lysias still licking their wounds from the near total defeat in the campaign against the territory of Yhuwdah (Judea). The peaceful compromise was like vomit in the mouth of Demetrius I Soter knowing his late uncle would be totally outraged. Therefore, he quickly devised a coup with his power and status and captured and killed Antiochus V Eupator and Viceroy Lysias. He then became king in Antioch and revised the old policies and statutes knowing that he now would have to face the upstart power of Rome and the stubborn will of the Hebrew people.

Back in the territory of Yhuwdah (Judea) that same year it found itself free from the external threat of enemies invading its land and attempting to take away their religious freedoms. Yhuwdah (Judas) Maccabim heard about the fame of the Romans that they were mighty and valiant men and would lovingly accept all that joined themselves unto them and make a league of amity with all that came. It was also told to him that all of Rome's enemies who refused their friendship of amity were utterly crushed and totally decimated. Yet, friends of Rome who kept their amity and helped the upstart Roman Republic with their cause of dominion, especially against the Helenes (Greeks) were allowed to remain peacefully in the kingdom of Rome. Yhuwdah was impressed with Rome's form of government which had a Senate House where three-hundred and twenty men met daily consulting how its dominion would maintain peaceful order. He also put in his mind that Rome and the territory of Yhuwdah (Judea) had a common enemy, the Grecians.

Therefore, Yhuwdah dispatched Eupolemus the son of Yowchanan (John) and Yhowshuwa (Joshua) also called Jason, the son of El'azar to Rome to testify before the great Senate House to make a league of amity and confederacy with them. After traveling the great journey they came before the Roman Senate to speak and said, "Yhuwdah Maccabim and his brothers and the people of the Hebrews have sent us to you to make a confederacy and peace with you and what we might be registered as your confederates and friends." This pleased the three-hundred and twenty members of the Roman Senate greatly because this would save the expense of a military campaign against "The Hebrew Hammer" to subdue it. A copy of their agreement was sent back to the great city of Yruwshalaim and read out loud by Yhuwdah (Judas) to the people. It was written on tablets of brass so the Hebrews could keep them as a memorial of peace and confederacy.

The inscription on the tablets read, "Good success be to the Romans and to the people of the Hebrews by sea and by land forever. Also may the sword and the enemy be far from them. If there come first any war upon the Romans or any of their confederates throughout all their dominion, then the people of the Hebrews shall help then as the time shall be appointed with all their heart. The Hebrew people shall not give those who stand against and make war with the Roman Republic any victuals, weapons, money or ships as it seems good to the Romans. But the Hebrew people shall keep their covenants. In the same manner also, if war comes first upon the nation of the Hebrews, the Roman Republic shall help them with all their heart according to the time that shall be appointed unto them. The Roman Republic shall not give to those who stand against and make war with the Hebrew people any victuals, weapons, money or ships as it seems good to the Romans, but shall keep their covenants without any deceit. According to these articles the Roman Republic make a covenant with the Hebrew people. However, if either party wants to add or subtract anything in this agreement then it must be ratified. As far as the touching evils that Demetrius I Soter, the betrayer of the Roman Republic, does to the Hebrew people to make the yoke heavy upon our friends and confederates, the Hebrew people we shall warn him that if you complain any more from coming against you, we shall do them justice and fight with you by sea and by land."

When Alcimus Yakim, the High Priest, heard that an alliance had been struck between Yhuwdah (Judea) and the Roman Republic even to fight against his Helene (Greek) heritage he became outraged. As *HaGadawl Kohen,* High Priest, he removed Menelaus as *kohen,* priest, and had him executed. Then he murdered sixty other *kohen,* priests, who opposed him. This put Alcimus in open conflict with the Maccabim family and began an internal struggle between the party of Hebrews led by Yhuwdah and the Hellenist party. Alcimus feared the Maccabim family he so he fled from the great city of Yruwshalaim and ran whimpering to king Demetrius I Soter in Antioch, asking for help.

The agreement with the Roman Republic and the Hebrew people failed to have any effect on the policy of Demetrius I Soter. He sympathized with Alcimus Yakim and assembled twenty-thousand footmen and two thousand horsemen and invaded Yhuwdah (Judea) and was met by "The Hebrew Hammer", Yhuwdah (Judas) Maccabim and his army at the village of Elasa (present day Ramallah) located eight miles north of the great city of Yruwshalaim. "The Hebrew Hammer" had with him three-thousand *gammedim*, warriors, but when the men saw that the Grecian armies were numerically so superior two-thousand of the men left the field of battle and advised their leader Yhuwdah (Judas) to do the same and await a more favorable opportunity. "The Hebrew Hammer" refused to retreat and stood his ground and met the Helene (Greek) phalanx formation head on. The *gammedim*, warriors of Yhuwdah scattered the two-thousand horsemen but the left wing of the phalanx formation hemmed him in on both sides and killed him. His brothers Shim'own (Simon) and Yownathan (Jonathan) took charge and defeated Demetrius I Soter sending him back to Antioch with his tail between his legs. However, the battle had cost the territory of Yhuwdah their spiritual and military commander, Yhuwdah (Judas) Maccabim, "The Hebrew Hammer". Shim'own (Simon) and Yownathan (Jonathan) removed his body from the battle field and buried him next to his father, Matityahu, in the valley village of Modi'im.

The Hebrew people encouraged Yownathan (Jonathan) Maccabim, nicknamed Apphus, meaning "The Diplomat" to assume the throne as military commander and *HaGadowl Kohen*, High Priest of the free territory of Yhuwdah (Judea). He was the youngest of the five sons of Matityahu but his reputation for courage was not questionable. Shortly following his brother's death, Yownathan (Jonathan) noticed that Bacchides, the Helene (Greek) general that killed Yhuwdah, "The Hebrew Hammer", was trying to entrap him. So he along with his brothers, Shim'own (Simon) and Yowchanan

(John) took some men and went to the desert region of Thecoe and camped near the pool of Asphar. Baccides followed him there and caught up with him on the Sabbath. Therefore, Yownathan (Jonathan) gave all their baggage into the hands of his brother Yowchanan (John) to take a small force and head towards the friendly Nabateans (Arabs) in order to secure the baggage. However, the sons of Yambri from the village town of Medaba, a hostile tribe of thieves, ambushed Yowchanan (John) killing him and his men and then looted the baggage.

Why would Satan's minions use the Arab town of Medaba to carry out this deception, thievery and murder? Was this just planting the seed for a far much grandeur plan for the death and destruction for mankind? Why was the world of darkness and evil rejoicing over the actions of this small and previously peaceful Arab city? Medaba was a city in Western Saudi Arabia near the coast of the Red Sea. It was virtually unnoticed until seven-hundred and thirty years later in 570 A.D this town of thieves would be called Mecca. Here, a son would be born to Abdallah son of Abdal Muttalib son of Hashim. His birth name was Abu al-Qasim Muhammad translated means, Father of the tribe of Qu'raish of the family of Hammad, but in history would only be known as Muhammad. Mecca became the most holy city for the religion of Islam, the largest eternal death trap for the entire Middle East and Europe attempting to spread its poisonous venom to all of mankind on the earth.

Yownathan (Jonathan) and his brother Shim'own heard the news about their brother Yowchanan (John) and engaged in battle with Bacchides and defeated him causing him to lose one-thousand men. Then the two brothers traveled outside of Medaba (Mecca) and hid in the hills. One of the sons of Yambri was leading home a noble bride from Nadabatha in great pomp with beating of drums and instruments of music. The great wedding procession was about three-hundred men. The Maccabim brothers ambushed the sons of Yambri and killed the entire party, getting their baggage back and avenging the death of their brother Yowchanan (John). They buried him near his brothers and father in the valley village of Modi'im. A period of peace began for the territory of Yhuwdah (Judea) and the great city of Yruwshalaim in 160 B.C.

Yownathan (Jonathan) took advantage of this period of peace and fortified the great city of Yruwshalaim in 153 B.C. restoring spiritual strength to the Hebrew people. Their oppressor king Demetrius I Soter who ruled in Antioch, Syria was murdered by the Arabs who beheaded him in 150 B.C. Light for total freedom as a nation once again began to dawn and shine brightly upon Yownathan Maccabim, The Diplomat. The dark clouds which had hung over this people for so long seemed to be lifting. Alexander Balas from a providence in western Turkey called Smyrna convinced the Roman Senate that he was the youngest son of Antiochus IV Epiphanes and the rightful heir to the throne in Antioch. The Roman Senate believed him along with king Ptolemy Philometor of Egypt, who gave him his daughter and made him king of Syria. Yownathan quickly used his diplomatic skills and sought peace with the new king of Syria, which was granted. He also gained diplomatic peace with Ptolemy Philometor of Egypt.

The light rays for the Hebrew people continued to gain strength against the dark clouds of evil which seemed to attempt to keep them in darkness instead of a pre-dawn light. The Roman Republic conquered Corinth Greece in 146 B.C. giving official control of their territories of Syria, Egypt and even Yhuwdah (Judea). However, the Roman Republic used a 'hands-off' policy in governing these new territories as long as they paid tribute to Rome. In 145 B.C.

Yownathan (Jonathan) Maccabim once again used his mounting power in the territory advanced the kingdom of Yahuah Yahusha by destroying the Dagon idols of the Philistines. However, his diplomatic ties to Syria were shaken a bit when Demetrius II Nicator claimed the throne in Syria from Alexander Balas. He was the son of the former enemy of the Hebrew people, Demetrius I Soter.

Yownathan (Jonathan) seized the opportunity to reestablish the Hebrew people as an independent nation knowing that he did not owe any allegiance to the new king of Syria. Therefore, he attacked the Grecian fortress in the great city of Yruwshalaim to rid the Hebrew people of the symbol of Helene (Greek) control over the territory of Yhuwdah (Judea). Demetrius II Nicator became incensed and appeared with an army outside of Yruwshalaim and ordered Yownathan to come before him. Yownathan accompanied by the elders and *koen*, priests, went to the new king and pacified him with presents. The king was so impressed with his diplomatic skills that he gave Yownathan more cities for the Hebrew people to control and confirmed him as the *HaGadowl Kohen*, High Priest, of the Hebrew people. Also, in consideration of a present of three-hundred talents the entire country was exempted from taxes, which was confirmed in writing. In return Yownathan lifted the siege against the Grecian fortress and garrison in Yruwshalaim and allowed the Helenes (Greeks) to stay.

Then in 143 B.C., a new claimant to the Grecian throne in Antioch, Syria appeared in person as the young Antiochus VI Dionysus, the son of Alexander Balas. He was only three-years-old but General Diodotus Tryphon used him to advance his own designs on the throne. In the face of this new enemy, Demetrius II Nicator not only promised Yownathan (Jonathan) that he would withdraw the garrison from the city of Yruwshalaim but also flattered him as his ally and requested the Hebrews to send troops to protect his throne. "The Diplomat" Yownathan honored the request and sent three-thousand men and protected King Demetrius II Nicator in his capital, Antioch, against his own subjects. However, after the Hebrew troops soundly defeated General Diodotus Tryphon and his troops, then King Demetrius II Nicator went back on his word. Thus early in 142 B.C. Yownathan being the expert politician that he was, thought it better to support a new king and allowed General Diodotus Tryphon and now four-year old Antiochus VI to seize Antioch and the throne. Also, by switching allegiance, Yownathan (Jonathan) bargained with General Diodotus Tryphon before the attack and the General was willing to confirm all of Yownathan previous rights and sweetened the 'deal' by appointing his brother Shim'own (Simon) as Strategos, the highest ranking officer from the Ladder of Tyre to the frontier of Egypt.

Yownathan and Shim'own were now entitled to make conquests with the blessings of Antioch so Yownathan renewed the treaty with the Roman Republic to also get their blessing. His diplomatic skills paid off as he and his brother conquered Gaza then Yownathan turned north and conquered as far north to the plain of Hazar in northeastern Turkey while Shim'own captured the strong fortress of Beyth-zur thirty miles south of Yruwshalaim, the strongest outpost and garrison in Yhuwdah (Judea). All seemed to be going well for the Hebrew people, maybe all too well. In the fall of 142 B.C. as Yownathan, his two sons, and forty-thousand *gammadim*, warriors, were returning from the far north and Shim'own was returning to the great city of Yruwshalaim from the south, the pre-dawn light began to disappear and be replaced with dark evil clouds. The Maccabim brothers would soon learn that this 'free hand' of independent power by the throne of Antioch, Syria was nothing but a deceptive ploy of wickedness with the intrigue of kidnapping and murder as the main plot. Satan's wicked plan of using governments to destroy the fellowship of Yahuah from His people was working as planned. The sting from the tails of the wicked demonic beasts into the governments of Roman and Grecian rule continued to inflict their poison of betrayal, greed, murder and an unquenchable thirst for power with the Hebrew people as the target.

With the two large Hebrew armies separated and feeling their oats from very successful military campaigns, General Diodotus Tryphon sent word from Antioch, Syria to Yownathan as he was returning from the north. The message was to meet the general for a friendly conference at the garrison of Ptolemais also called Acre located eighty miles northwest of Yruwshalaim on the Mediterranean Sea Coast, promising to finally turn over the garrison to Yownathan. "The Diplomat" was elated that the throne in Antioch was going to remove this garrison from the sight of Yrushalalim as had been promised many times and turn control over to the Hebrew people. Therefore, Yownathan dismissed thirty-seven thousand *gammedim*, warriors, sent two-thousand into the nearby territory of Galilee and kept one-thousand men to go with him to the garrison. He also dispatched word to Yruwshalaim to give to his brother Shim'own who was returning from the south, that he would be slightly delayed since he was going to take control of the garrison at Acre from the Helenes (Greeks).

As soon as Yownathan (Jonathan) arrived inside the garrison gates, the gates were slammed shut and flying arrows rained down from the sky. The surprised one-thousand man army of Yownathan was in the middle of an ambush and those nearest to Yownathan and his two sons covered them with their shields and bodies. Their horses discarded the Hebrew soldiers and fled, trampling men underfoot as they escaped. Yownathan tried to gain control of the chaos but the screams of his dying soldiers was so loud no one could hear his commands. As the stinging arrows found their mark more and more of the Hebrew shields dropped that provided scarce protection. When the will to fight left those who remained, long spears and swords descended upon them like a title wave. In the end, all were killed except Yownathan and his two sons accompanying him. Yownathan and his sons were taken prisoners and held hostage with a message sent to his brother Shim'own who just arrived back in the great city of Yruwshalaim demanding one-hundred talents of silver owed to the king's treasury in Antioch, Syria for conducting business with the throne. Shim'own did not trust General Diodotus Tryphon assuming that in reality it was a trap and that the general's real intention was to invade Yhuwdah (Judea). Fearing a mighty armored invasion of the Hebrew territory, the men of Yruwshalaim shrunk with great fear.

7

Then Shim'own said to all the assembled people, "Hebrew brothers, you know what great things my brothers and I and my father's house have done for the Law and the Sanctuary of the Temple. Also, you know the battles and troubles that we have seen. For some reason all my brothers have been slain for the sake of our Hebrew nation, Yisra'Yah (Israel) except for Yownathan and now his life may be in danger, if not already dead. At this time, only I am left alive. Therefore, far be it for me that I should spare my own life in time of trouble because I am no better than my brothers. Have no doubt that I will avenge my nation, the Sanctuary, our wives and our children. With the hand of Yahuah and you at my side we will destroy all the heathen that have gathered against us for malice."

This rousing speech mustered a mighty army of *gammedim*, warriors, including the thirty-seven thousand men who had just returned from marching north with Yownathan (Jonathan). The ground literally shook with the multiple thousands of footmen, chariots and cavalry of the Hebrews as they headed north to the garrison of Acre. When General Diodotus Tryphon realized that Shim'own did not take the bait of the ransom demands and instead rallied a crushing army, he emptied and abandoned the garrison retreating back to Antioch, Syria. However, a heavy snow fell and stopped the hasty retreat. Knowing he could not defeat Shim'own and his army, he murdered Yownathan and his sons and put them in shallow graves with markers as a ploy hoping that when seeing the markers Shim'own would call off the hunt and grieve for his brother and nephews. The demonic plot did not work but had the opposite effect. When Shim'own and his army found the graves they picked up the pace and engaged in battle with the general sending him back to Antioch with a very few surviving men and deeply crushed. Then Shim'own returned and dug up the bones of Yownathan (Jonathan) and his two sons and buried them in the valley village of Modi'im. Now in the late winter of 142 B.C. Shim'own (Simon) Maccabim took on the responsibility of being the *HaGadowl Kohen,* High Priest, for the Hebrew people.

After the first of the year in 141 B.C., to honor the Maccabim family for their dedication to the Hebrew nation, it was established by formal decree at a large assembly of the *kohen* (priests), the Hebrew people and the elders of the land, that the Maccabim name should be considered a royal family of Yisra'Yah and that the royal name should bear the name of Shim'own's great-great-grandfather Asmon. Thus the Maccabim rule would be called the Hasmonean Dynasty. Furthermore it stated to the effect that Shim'own (Simon) Maccabim should be their leader and *HaGadowl Kohen* (High Priest) forever, until there should arise a faithful prophet.

As the coronation of a new leader was taking place in territory of Yhuwah (Judea) by the Hebrew people, back in Antioch, Syria General Diodotus Tryphon crowned himself as king and assassinated the five-year old king Antiochus VI, son of Alexander Balas. In the spring of 141 B.C. when Shim'own heard this news he sent word to Demetrius II Nicator, the previous king, that he would consider an alliance with him and help him regain control of the throne in Antioch, Syria if Demetrius II Nicator first killed Diodotrus Tryphon. Diodotus Tryphon got word of this possible new alliance tainted with revenge for the blood of Yownathan (Jonathan) Maccabim and his two sons and quickly abdicated the throne, and fled to the wilderness. Demetrius II Nicator regained the throne in Antioch, Syria and sent his son Antiochus VII and General Ptolomee, son of Abubus with thirty-thousand men to join forces with ten-thousand Hebrew *gammedim,* warriors, commanded by Yowchanan (John) Hyrcanus I, the oldest son of Shim'own (Simon) Maccabim to hunt down and kill Diodotus Tryphon. The allied forces of the Hebrews and the Syrians caught up with the coward ex-general and in fierce fighting killed him and all of his twenty-eight thousand soldiers and cavalry. This avenged the blood for the Hebrew people and solidified the throne in Antioch, Syria for Demetrius II Nicator a newly acquired ally for Shim'own Maccabim. This alliance meant a period of peace for the Hebrew people and the ruling power of the Hasmonean Dynasty. To solidify the alliance with Antioch, Shim'own (Simon) gave his daughter in marriage to General Ptolomee. A short time after the wedding, King Demetrius II Nicator came down with a high fever and died.

The air was thick with eerie screaming and haunted laughing from the demonic beasts that Satan sent to deceive the world governments of Rome and Grecian controlled Syria. Why were they rejoicing? They had just lost one of their evil henchmen in ex-general Diodotus Tryphon. Also, King Demetrius II Nicator of Syria had betrayed the Maccabim family once before when it was ruled by Yownathan Maccabim. In addition, the young Roman Republic was an ally to the Hebrews, not an invading taskmaster. The territory of Yhuwdah was at peace and not enslaved by constant invasions and threats on denying worship to Yahuah Yahusha. The great city of Yruwshalaim was controlled by the Hebrews and not a foreign nation, so why all the evil demonic celebration? What evil concoction was Satan cooking up next? Was this calm that the Hebrew people were experiencing a sadistic trick of some kind? Were they really going to be allowed to rebuild a relationship of restored fellowship with Creator Yahuah Yahusha? Would the Hebrew people finally be allowed to lead the rest of mankind in the world to the throne of the King of kings and Lord of lords? Was Satan finally defeated, if so why the putrid party by the demonic beasts?

Antiochus VII Sidetes, the son of Demetrius II Nicator assumed the crown and throne in Antioch, Syria of his father with the blessings of Rome and Shim'own (Simon) Maccabim of Yhuwdah (Judea). Antiochus VII appointed his general Ptolomee, son of Abubus as governor of the city of Yriychow (Jericho). This pleased Shim'own very much because that put his only daughter and his new-son-in-law just twenty-two miles to the northeast of the great city of Yruwshalaim. Shim'own nicknamed Thassi, The Zealous, was a very just and righteous ruler of the Hebrew people. He also never forgot the diplomatic skills of his late brother Yownathan (Jonathan). Therefore, he sent a delegation to the Roman Senate in Rome to renew the alliance that was agreed upon with his brother Yownathan. *HaGadowl Kohen*, High Priest, and leader of the Hebrew people selected Numenius, the son of King Antiochus VII to be the head of the delegation. The Roman Senate welcomed Numenius with open arms and was pleased to listen to a representative who had ties to the throne in Antioch, Syria and also the authority of an old ally from the territory of Yhuwdah (Judea). In 139 B.C. the Roman Senate overwhelmingly approved the renewing of the previous agreement with the new leader Shim'own Maccabim. The Roman Senate even went a step further declaring that the newly recognized Hasmonean Dynasty could rule the Hebrew people semi-independent of the throne in Antioch, Syria.

Five years later, 135 B.C., after ruling in peace in the territory of

Yhuwdah (Judea) for seven years, Shim'own (Simon) called his three sons together on the 4th day of the month of Tevet (late December) following the final day of the eight consecutive day celebration of the Feast of Dedication called *Chanukah*, Hanukkah (Festival of Lights). He said to them, "I and my dead brothers and my father's house have even from our youth until this day have fought against the enemies of Yisra" Yah (Israel). Things have prospered so well in our hands that we have delivered this nation many times. Now, my sons, I am very old. My once sharp mind and muscled body have grown very weary and ache daily. Yet, by Yahuah's mercy I am still alive and an effective ruler at this ripe old age. Today, I appoint my oldest son, Yhowchanan Hyrcanus I as the new leader of the Hebrew people and Yhuwdah and Mattathias will serve as his generals. I will serve only as the *HaGadowl Koen,* High Priest, and intend to do so as long as I am physically capable to be a servant of Yahuah. I will notify the political party of the *Chaciydim*, Hasidim in the morning. Now, go forth and fight for our nation and the Law and Commandments of Yahuah when they are threatened with violence and may the help of Heaven be with you."

The following week, the first week of the new year of 134 B.C., a courier from the city of Yriychow (Jericho) came riding as it left a trail of dust and entered through the gates of the great city of Yruwshalaim (Jerusalem). The tap-tap-tap from the hooves of the horse could be heard all the way up to the Hasmonean Palace. Breathless, the messenger urged the servant to fetch Shim'own (Simon) Maccabim immediately as he had an urgent message from his son-in-law, Ptolomee, son of Abubus and could only be delivered in person. The servant hurried into the main gate of the house and did as the young messenger had requested. Shim'own (Simon) came as fast as his aged legs could carry him hoping that it was not bad news. Thoughts quickly sifted through his weary mind as he made his way to the patiently waiting royal courier. *Is the city of Yrichow (Jericho) under siege? Is my precious daughter Diynah in poor health? Is the territory of Yhuwdah (Judah) being invaded once again? Did something tragic happen to King Antiochus VII Sidetes, in Antioch, Syria? Was the young Roman Republic under attack in Rome?* All these thoughts of anxiousness caused beads of sweat to form on the forehead of Shim'own. Then the sweat ran down his cheeks into his long white beard. The royal courier bowed his head as Shim'own approached and held out the sealed scroll of parchment.

Shim'own acknowledged the young courier and said, "Shalom." The young courier continued to hold onto the leather reigns of his horse in his right hand. The horse snorted and shook his drenched lathered neck as its withers caved in and out trying to catch its breath. The young courier nodded his head and let go of his delivery that was outstretched in his left hand. Then he waited patiently to see if there would be a reply to return back to the city of Yriychow (Jericho) to his master the governor. Shim'own quickly broke the seal and grabbed the top of the scroll with his right hand and the bottom of the scroll with his left hand and began to unroll the parchment with care. By now the palace courtyard was all abuzz about the sudden commotion as a great audience had gathered with many sets of eyes fixed on the face of *HaGadowl Kohen*, High Priest, Shim'own. His three sons also had been summoned by curious servants and their presence was now trying to peer over Shim'own's shoulders to get a glance at the document with their own eyes.

Shim'own stopped unrolling the parchment and said, "Ok, get back and give an old man space to breathe. I will read the letter out loud to you so all will know of this critical and important news." His sons stepped back and the servants chuckled quietly as they enjoyed seeing the old man still able to put his sons in their place. Shim'own cleared his throat and began unrolling the scroll again reading it out loud, *"Honorable Father-in-law, Shim'own Maccabim being HaGadowl Kohen of the Hebrew people, greetings of peace from the strong city of Yriychow. I also send the love of your beautiful daughter, Diynah who also has news of her own to share with you. First, I shall address business and then I will get to the personal messages."* Shim'own continued to unroll the scroll with his left hand and roll it back up with his right hand as he read the parchment out loud.

"As governor of Yriychow I have learned about the recent leadership changes from the great city of Yruwshalaim for the Hebrew territory of Yhuwdah. I support your decision to step down as the leader and give the responsibility to Yhowchanan Hyrcanus I. You have fought enough struggles and agonized mentally over many battles and now it is time to rest the mental strain. You have provided peaceful leadership free from conflict and invasion for your Hebrew people going on seven years now. You need to be commended for accomplishing this daunting task. Your trustworthy alliances with the Roman Republic in Rome and the throne in Antioch, Syria are invaluable and are a credit to your great leadership and deep wisdom. It is time to honor the man that accomplished so much with so little resources."

"Therefore, I, Ptolomee, son of Abubus, High Governor of Yriychow invite and request the presence of you and your sons as special guests to a banquet that I wish to hold in your honor in one month, the month of Shabat (February). I intend for the menu to include: Roasted Pheasant and Quail surrounded with slices of fresh Oranges and Lemons; Roasted Beef fattened on the lush green pastures of Bashan smothered in boiled Carrots, Potatoes and Onions brought from Mitsrayim (Egypt); Round Loaves of freshly baked Bread; Sliced Apples from the fruit orchards of Golan Heights dipped

in the sticky-gummy syrup of *Honey from the beehives of Gaza; Sweet Melon Cubes from the Royal Garden of Watermelon, Muskmelon and Honey Dew Melon; Freshly Cracked Almonds and Cashews; Black and Green Olives from Galilee; (and as a personal surprise to your liking) unlimited supply of fresh Fine Wine from the vineyards of the valley village of Modi'im and blocks of Yellow and White Cheeses and large bowls of Tantalizing Curds made from the milk of the vast goat herds of Modi'im, the hometown of the Maccabim family."*

"Now if I haven't tempted you with your stomach then the personal news of your beautiful daughter will propel you and her brothers to pay us a visit in order to honor the greatest leader of the Hebrew people since King David. Diynah sends word that you will become a grandfather! I hope you will stay a few days with us following the banquet. I respectfully request that you please send word back with my royal courier in order that I may start the preparations right away. I anxiously await your reply in the acceptance of my humble invitation. Signed your devoted son-in-law, High Governor of Yriychow, Ptolomee, son of Abubus."

A huge smile from ear to ear was exhibited on the face of Shim'own creating a large valley between his white beard and white mustache. It was like a wide valley in the white snow covered mountains of Lebanon. Then all his bottled up emotions exploded into an exclamation of, *"Halal Yah*, Celebrate to Yahuah!" This was followed by spontaneous and continous laughter and slapping on the backs of those gawking spectators in the courtyard. Even some of the curious passerby's on the cobblestone street in front of the palace, stopped and joined in the joyous celebration. Some of the male servants even locked forearms and began round dancing and kicking up their legs. The only thing that paused the celebration was the young courier holding onto his horse when he yelled above the commotion, "Is there a reply, Honored *Kohen*?" Shim'own paused his skipping and dancing and with laughter gently grabbed the young courier's shoulder and said, "Tell my son-in-law, Governor Ptolomee that I am humbly honored and will enthusiastically accept his invitation." At that, the royal courier mounted his horse and galloped down the street towards the gate leading north back to the city of Yriychow (Jericho).

Yhowchanan Hyrcanus I, informed his father that he would not be able to accompany him and be a guest at the gala banquet. He had pressing matters to attend to concerning the political party of the *Chaciydim*, Hasidim. Therefore, when the time came, a small caravan left the North Gate headed northeast on the dusty road towards the city of Yriychow. The caravan included camels carrying expensive gifts for the Governor and special gifts for his wife, Diynah, the daughter of Shim'own. The personal body guards and servants of Shim'own accompanied him along with his two sons, Yhuwdah and Mattathias. The pre-dawn light was just peaking over the horizon as they had decided to get an early start to arrive in plenty of time for the evening banquet. Those twenty-two long miles could not come soon enough for the aged old *koen*, priest as the invitation had put a noticeable spring in his step and he acted with the impatience of a twenty-year old young man.

As they entered the gates of the city of Yriychow (Jericho), brass trumpets sounded and the flapping of many banners lined the main thoroughfare leading to the Governor's palace. Cheers and applause erupted from those on both sides of the street and the eyes of Shim'one became clouded over with the moisture of tears as he realized all this was for him. He lifted his head and said, "All praise and honor belong to You, Yahuah, as it was the work of Your hand that accomplished the impossible tasks of my father and brothers." Soon they arrived at the end of the lane and the Governor and his wife Diynah met them with kisses and bear hugs. Then Ptolomee, Governor and son-in-law of Shim'own scanned the group of travelers and said, "Where is Yhowchanan Hyrcanus I? Did he refuse my invitation?" Shim'own detected a twinge of irritation in the voice of Ptolomee but then thought it was his own imagination and replied, "In all the excitement I almost forgot to mention to you that Yhowchanan sends his deepest regrets and apologies for not making the trip but official government business keeps him tied up in the great city of Yruwshalaim. However, he does send his cordial greetings and wishes that you accept his sincere apology of missing such a grand celebration."

After their cordial and joyous greetings, Shim'own and his sons retired to their guest rooms to change from their dirty travel clothes to put on their banquet attire. Succulent smells permeated the halls of the palace as the final touches were being put on the vast and abundant banquet of food and fine wine. Musicians began playing their harmonious instruments, and house servants scampered about getting things ready on the long tables of food. The entertainment for the banquet had just arrived and they were being given their final instructions. The banquet of honor was finally ready and the evening gong began calling the guests with is hollow vibrations. Guests were seated according to their importance but Shim'own noticed that his daughter was not present.

Shim'own greeted Governor Ptolomee leaning to his ear said, "Will my daughter be joining us tonight for the celebration?" Ptolomee smiled and responded, "Maybe later after the banquet, she had a slight headache and was fearful that the boisterous laughing of the guests would cause it to worsen." Then they all began to inhale the mouth-watering cuisine stuffing their mouths and bellies as if there would not be a tomorrow. The fine wine of Modi'im flowed freely like a constant bubbling brook and lightened the spirits of those in attendance. When Shim'own, the Governor's father-in-law and his two brother-in-laws had drunk largely on the wine and they were feeling gleeful, it was time to honor Shim'own with special presents. Three male servants carried gifts bearing them on silk pillows and stood behind the three honored guests.

Once again the demonic beasts began their wild eerie laughter and haunting screams. The wickedness of their world that hovered over Rome and the Middle East was like a hungry vulture searching for death so it could savor its next meal. Why were these minions celebrating that a Hebrew man was being honored for constantly defeating their master, Satan, the eternal enemy of Yahuah Yahusha? Did they not inject their venom from their tails into the opposing governments of the Hebrews to incite betrayal, greed, murder and an unquenchable thirst for power? Should they not be whimpering in defeat and howling because of their constant failure to bring Rome and Grecian controlled Syria against the Hebrew nation of Yisra'Yah (Israel)? Did the constant inhalation of the putrid odor of burning sulfur and decaying flesh cloud their sense of reality? To this point they had failed except for the kidnapping and murder of Yownathan (Jonathan) Maccabim. However, his blood had been revenged and his brother Shim'own, the main guest of honor, who had ruled in virtual peace for seven years without the evil beasts being able to sink their bloody talons or spread their poisonous venom into mankind to conspire against the nation of Yisra'Yah. Was this a conspiracy concocted by Satan all along to lure the righteous into his wicked death trap? How could this festive and joyous banquet planned by the Governor Ptolomee, the son of Abubus, the son-in-law of the guest of honor bring such happiness with the dark lord of death, destruction and his multitudes of demonic minions hovering over the Middle East looking for treachery?

Then Governor Ptolomee, son of Abubus raised his goblet and said, "Everyone raise their wine goblet as I toast my father-in-law in whose honor this fine banquet is given. Honored Shim'own, these goblets were specially made from your town of origin, the valley village of Modi'im where the effervescent liquid that filled these goblets was made. You may remember a small young boy many years ago from Modi'im by the name of Ya'aqob (Jacob), the son of the tin maker. His father died and he continues his family's occupation as tin maker. He is the little boy who brought Commander Hippokrates to the front doorstep of your father's house. The lad's guiding light put many events into motion that began the "Maccabim Revolt" and set the Hasmonean Dynasty as the leadership power of the Hebrew people that still exists to this very day thirty-three years later...." Then Ptolomee, son of Abubus smiled at his father-in-in law and bowed his head in honor. Just as he bowed his head the three servants drew daggers from inside the silk pillows and slit the throats of Shim'own Maccabim and his two sons Yhuwdah and Mattathias. The paid guests who attended were sworn to secrecy by Governor Ptolomee upon death if their silence was broken to expose what happened. Thus, all the Maccabim who had begun the revolt for the freedom of worship to Yahuah Yahusha by His Law and His Commandments were now dead in 134 B.C. The death vulture smiled as Maccabim blood dripped from his long sharp talons.

8

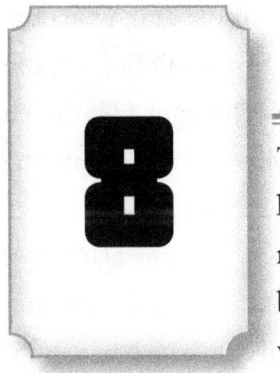

The poison of betrayal, murder, greed, and lust for power was just taking its effect as it ran through the growing-cold veins of the blood of mankind. The hideous beasts now were working overtime to please their dark lord Satan and began to cast a long dark shadow over mankind and began to obscure the fellowship of mankind with Yahuah Yahusha. The air over the Roman Republic and the Middle East was saturated with eerie screams and haunting hissing as the minion beasts spread their poison brought from the evil smoking cauldron of Satan's devilish Hell. What was in store for the earthly inhabitants as Satan tried to blot out the pre-dawn light? How much more flesh did the death vulture require of the righteous until it got is complete fill of death and destruction? Would the foundation of righteousness and defending the Law and Commandments of Yahuah that Matityahu Maccabim and his five sons laid begin to crumble or would it stand? If it did stand would it grow stronger or would it weaken?

Yhowchanan Hyrcanus I received the surname of Hyrcanus I because when he was the chief general of the military command under the administration of his father, Shim'own Maccabim, he was stationed at the ancient fortress garrison of Hyrcania. Hyrcania was located in Yhuwdah Desert of the West Bank sixteen miles east of the great city of Yruwshalaim. He fought alongside Antiochus VII Sidetes in a campaign which resulted in the release of Antiochus' brother Antiochus VIII Gryphos from captivity. That was seven years ago. Now in 134 B.C. he is the Leader of the Hebrew people living in peace semi-independently from the throne in Antioch, Syria. It had been only a day since his father had been gone to the grand banquet thrown in his honor by Yowchanan's brother-in-law, Ptolomee, son of Abubus the Governor of the city of Yriychow (Jericho). He wanted to seek his father's council concerning the political matters that the *Chaciydim*, Hasidim had proposed to him yesterday, since they were really mostly religious concerns and Shim'own was the *HaGadowl Kohen*, High Priest, of the Hebrew people. As he paced back and forth in front of the north window watching deep in the horizon for a cloud of dust from the returning caravan, he finally remembered that his father and two younger brothers had been invited to stay an extra day following the banquet. Then Yhowchanan Hyrcanus I slapped his hands together and said to himself, *I shall go ask my mother as she knows the mind of my father better than anyone.* This brought a big smile to his previous tense and anxious face. Now his countenance was light and cheerful as he quickly strode with a skip in his steps to the main Hasmonean Palace to see his mother.

The constant rhythm of the beating of his sandals on the cobble stones of the street made a clop-clop sound and only ended when he arrived at the front gate. There he was met by the main gatekeeper and Yhowchanan Hyrcanus I said, "Shalom. Is my mother in the Palace?" The gatekeeper replied, "No, young master. She left last night with four of the Governor's men from the city of Yriychow." Yhowchanan Hyrcanus I was puzzled and thought *why would she go to Yriychow last night when she knew that father would be returning home later this evening?* So he continued to interrogate the main gatekeeper, "Was there an emergency? Did something happen to my father or my brothers? Is my sister ok with her expecting child? What was so important that she would not inform me that she was leaving?" "Take a breath young master. I can't answer these questions because I am only the lowly gatekeeper letting people in and letting them out. Let me fetch her main servant in the house," said the man. Realizing his frustration Yhowchanan Hyrcanus I said, "Never mind gatekeeper. I am sorry to burden you with all these questions. I should have thought about old Hagar myself. Thank you for your help and I will let you get back to your duty." The gatekeeper nodded and said, "Very well young master. I believe that Hagar is tending to the daily laundry at the present time. You might check the washhouse."

Yhowchanan Hyrcanus I decided to take a shortcut instead of going through the drab servants quarters so he quickly strode through the lush green manicured lawn surrounding the courtyard of the palace. He then went through the arched lattice work gate which led to the royal flower garden. The aromatic aroma of the large varietal of blooming flowers was sweet to smell and the beauty of the multi-colored pinks, reds, yellows, oranges, blues, and violets was like a stroll through a garden equal to that of ancient Eden. It was like Yahuah Yahusha had painted a beautiful sunset of different hues on the ground. The garden contained several fountains of spewing water and gently falling waterfalls fed by water aqueducts supplied by springs just outside the city walls. On the other side of the garden was another lattice work gate that led to the back of the servants' quarters. Here he should find Hagar at the washhouse.

He went through the back gate and latched it and hollered out, "Hagar, Hagar where are you? Come here at once!" Around the corner came a slightly hunched aged woman carrying a wooden rug beater in her right hand. Her dark brown outer garment was covered with a smattering of white chalky dust. "Yhowchanan Hyrcanus I, don't you use that tone of voice with me. You are not old enough that I still won't use this beater on your backside. I have done it plenty of times before even if your mother had not requested it!" quipped the old woman. Yowchanan Hyrcanus I cowered down a bit and in a lower and much calmer voice said, "How well I remember woman, but I did not come here to discuss my childhood discipline with you. Why did my mother leave so suddenly last night to go to the city of Yriychow (Jericho)?" Hagar answered, "As you know, young master it is not proper for a fine Hebrew woman, to attend a banquet of wandering eyed men. Therefore, your sister invited your mother for a ladies banquet next week while the men were back to their normal daily life activities thus allowing your mother and sister to have social time not set by a male clock or schedule. That is why she did not travel with your father and two brothers yesterday morning."

"Hagar enough of the jib-chatter! Tell me why my mother went to Yriychow last night!" raised the voice of Yhowchanan Hyrcanus I. Hagar lifted the broom beater above her head, "Patience young master or I will swat your backside like an unwanted horsefly buzzing around my head. As a matter of fact, remember the time….." Yhowchanan Hyrcanus I interrupted and said, "My apologies wise and powerful queen of the far-reaching swatter and punisher of little boys who are full of mischief and misbehavior." At that they both giggled a little bit. Then Yhowchanan Hyrcanus I pleaded, "I am just concerned about my mother because this is not like her." Hagar lowered her well-used weapon that with its generational reputation of being worn out on the backsides of Maccabim boys more than on dusty rugs and said, "This is why your mother did not come to you last night because you know that you always have a habit of making a mountain out of a mole hill and you would worry yourself with fright. Your mother was requested by your brother-in-law, Governor Ptolomee, son of Abubus, to be present for a special surprise for your father. He was afraid that she would slip and tell your father because as you know they tell each other everything and this house has never been able to surprise them. However, the Governor wanted her present when he made a special announcement about a career advancement that he was to accept today in a special ceremony. So she left quickly with the heavily armed royal soldiers so as not to disappoint your father. Now, you get back to your office and quit all this worrying." With that she gave him a little pinch on the right cheek and tapped the tip of his nose softly with her forefinger. Yowchanan Hyrcanus I turned and headed back to the main gate feeling relieved.

Just as the main gatekeeper opened the gates to let Yhowchanan Hyrcanus I out onto the cobble stoned streets, in barged a breathless young man covered with limestone dust and perspiration. Startled, Yhowchanan Hyracnus I exclaimed, "What is the meaning of this?" As the main gatekeeper was drawing his sword, the breathless young man stammered, "Pardon your majesty, but I have terrible news about your family from the city of Yryichow." The main gatekeeper placed the point of his sharp sword under the chin of the breathless young man, placing himself between the perpetrator and Yhowchanan Hyrcanus I. The breathless young man continued as he felt the cold steel next to his throat, "I am Yowceph (Joseph) from the town of Gazara where you, your wife and two boys live. I was in Yriychow yesterday on business for my father and heard the news from last night. I snuck over the wall and ran here as fast as I could to warn you." Yhowchanan Hyrcanus I placed his hand on the main gatekeeper's sword indicating for him to lower it away from the young man's tender throat and then said, "Go on, tell me what news you have heard."

Yowceph continued, "Governor Ptolomee, son of Abubus, your brother-in-law intended the banquet of honor as a trap to kill your father, yourself and your two brothers so that he could expand his territory to the entire region of Yhuwdah instead of just the city of

Yriychow. However, you did not show up therefore he has murdered your father and two brothers and has taken your mother as hostage in order to kill you. He is massing a mighty army as we speak to invade Yhuwdah seeking to kill you and your sons. I fear for our little town and my family. As you know, it is not walled and is not defendable against a mighty siege. Please, I implore you lord Yhowchanan Hyrcanus I save our village and your family's life."

Upon hearing this news, Yhowchanan Hyrcanus I tore his outer robe and exclaimed, "*Carah*, apostasy!" Then he collapsed to the ground in grief and agony weeping uncontrollably. The main gatekeeper quickly sounded the warning trumpet of a curved ram's horn with a long continues blast. In a matter of time all the gates to the city of Yruwshalaim were shut and barred with no one coming in and no one going out. The news spread like a kindled wildfire being blown by the changing winds of rumors and fanned the burning flames higher and higher as mere moments of time took place. Military commanders quickly assembled on the courthouse lawn of the palace and the entire city was set on pins and needles when they learned of the news from the city of Yriychow. Even the *Chaciydim*, Hasidim pushed their way through the common folk in order to get into the palace courtyard to find out if the rumors were true. Their important political ambitions that were just discussed yesterday with Yhowchanan Hyrcanus I now hung on a balance since their key component was to be Shim'own Maccabim the *HaGadowl Kohen*, High Priest. Yhowchanan Hyrcanus I gained his composure and convened his war cabinet inside the large foyer of his father's living quarters. The decision was final, quick and unanimous as military commanders scurried like red ants on an anthill when something has intruded their territory.

By late afternoon, eighty-seven thousand *gammedim*, warriors, three-hundred chariots, two-thousand bowmen and a cavalry of six-thousand horses and riders were assembled and ready to march twenty-two miles northeast of the great city of Yruwshalaim to lay siege to the city of Yriychow (Jericho) and rescue the queen and mother of Yhowchanan Hyrcanus I and execute Ptolomee, son of Abubus, for murdering his father-in-law Shim'own and the two brothers of Yhowchanan Hyrcanus I. They would march through the night and prepare for attack formation on the east side of the city so that when the pre-dawn sun would rise in the east its light rays would cause a blinding light on all the armor of the Hebrews allowing for three large divisions to encircle behind the city as they would be hidden in the blinding light and they would not appear until they were in their final positions. The men would have a half of a nights rest so they would be rested and ready for battle.

The early morning hours came as darkness gave way to the pre-dawn light coming from the east. The sky was still dark except for a sliver of light peeking out of the darkness in the east making the sky blood red. A blood red sky in the morning was a bad omen as it meant that innocent blood had been shed and vengeance would pay for the innocent blood spilled before the sun set in the western horizon that very day. The watchmen in the eastern towers of the city of Yriychow watched the sliver of red grow larger in the eastern sky as the pre-dawn light was preparing to give birth to the light of a new day. Just below the ever growing red sky was a stationary shining object. "Probably a caravan breaking camp so they can be first to enter the city gates when we open them up soon," remarked one of the watchmen as he nudged the other one to sound the first hour call of the day (6:00 a.m.) which officially ended the fourth watch of the night. The call was sounded and the two weary-eyed watchmen traded places with fresh men for the first watch of the day.

By the time the new arrivals were situated for their watch the outline of the sun was just peeking over the horizon and that little shining object was now a growing blinding glare making it hard to see towards the east even when they squinted their eyes. The city gates were now open but the object of the light did not get any closer. It just grew larger and brighter. Thirty-minutes later, one of the watchmen sounded the alarm as the entire city seemed to be enclosed with this magical and mystical circle of bright light. The city gates were closed and barred and the sleepy city began to stir with sporadic commotion like a drunkard being awakened suddenly from a deep sleep, snorting and mumbling. Governor Ptolomee, son of Abubus, rolled quickly out of his bed, grabbed a robe and peered out his bedroom window at the noise from the growing panic in the city of Yriychow. Governor Ptolomee summoned his personal servant and inquired what the source of the commotion was. The servant filled him in about the mysterious circle of light surrounding the city and the people were afraid the gods were going to lay seige on the strong city or that maybe Yhowshuwa (Joshua) and the Hebrew people had been reincarnated as light and were attacking the city like they did over twelve-hundred and sixty years earlier. "Preposterous," snorted a now irritated governor, "Get my mother-in-law the prisoner and have her taken and bound on the eastern turret of the castle. I will be fully dressed and will meet you there in ten minutes so hurry!"

The early morning eastern sun had been birthed in the pre-dawn light and cast a blinding glow upon the whole city. The governor ran up the many winding steps to the eastern turret of the castle and smiled with a deceitful cunning smile towards his mother-in-law and then put his hands upon the ledge of turret. Then from out of the circling blinding light came a single flicker. It was a lone horseman carrying the royal Hebrew banner heading just below where the governor was holding Yhowchanan Hyrcanus I's mother hostage. The rider stopped and began to herald in a loud voice, "Governor Ptolomee, son of Abubus, I, Yhowchanan (John) Hyrcanus I, governmental authority of the territory of Yhuwdah and the Hebrew People, have come to investigate the rumors that have come to my ears and demand an answer. It has been said that you have murdered my father and two brothers, kidnapped and hold my mother as prisoner and the life of my little and only sister, your wife, is in danger! If my family does not exit your western gates alive and unharmed before the one-hundredth drum beat, I and the nation of Yhuwdah (Judea) will tear your strong city apart log from log and stone from stone until it is a dung heap!" Then the rider wheeled around and galloped back to the circle of light that grew brighter each passing minute and was swallowed out of eyesight into the bright glow. The people of the city of Yriychow panicked and began screaming for the governor to surrender.

Shim'own's widow smiled and said to the governor, "Yahuah has judged you today for your wickedness and *carah*, apostasy. You have been doomed to Sh'owl, the underworld of the dead." At that the governor slapped his mother-in-law across the mouth with a quick and mighty backhand that caused her head to snap sideways leaving blood trickling from the side of her mouth. He then turned to his royal scribe and had him jot a note to deliver to his brother-in-law Yhowchanan Hyrcanus I. Seventy-five steady drum beats had now gone by as one of the eastern gates was opened slightly and the dead and decomposing bodies of Shim'own and his two sons were cast outside with the gates quickly being re-shut and barred once again. The drums continued to beat as a company of chariots hurried to the discarded bodies. With great care they loaded the lifeless bodies on the chariots and returned to the circle of fire as the one-hundredth beat sounded on the drums. The identity of the bodies was revealed and the note attached to the robe of Shim'own was handed with downcast eyes to Yhowchanan Hyrcanus I. Then he read the note to his military commanders.

"Hyrcanus, you are nothing but a pious pig trying to oink and grunting at something that you can't and will not achieve. If you had not refused my invitation to the banquet then you could have joined your father and brothers in an honorable death instead of a crushing defeat on the battlefield with your name taken down to Sh'owl, the underworld of the dead in shame. Here is what is going to happen. You will turn tail and run back to the city of Yruwshalaim like the yellow-bellied coward that you are and call off this attack or I will torture your mother with each and every advancing step of your army! See you in Yruwshalaim where next time I will own you and your stubborn people and after I turn your city into a dung heap and reign as Yhuwdah's sovereign then I will release your mother, but you will be dead." Yhowchanan's rage boiled over as he crumpled the parchment and threw it to the ground. His company quickly rode to the front of the eastern formation where he could see his mother standing bound surrounded by the governor in the front peering over the wall of the turret and a guard on each side. As his company began to advance, Governor Ptolomee turned towards his mother and she wailed in response with a loud scream. Yhowchanan Hyrcanus I stopped the company and he could hear his mother begging him to attack the city of Yriychow and avenge the blood of his father and brothers. Each time he began to advance towards the city walls, he was stopped by the screams of painful torture of his mother. After several hours of standoff and listening to his weakening mother cry in agonizing pain and the heat of the noonday sun beating down upon his army, he turned and retreated back to the great city of

Yruwshalaim carrying the three dead bodies of his father and his two brothers. That night his mother and his sister were executed and their headless bodies were sent to the great city of Yruwshalaim as a 'trophy' to remind Yhowchanan Hyrcanus I of his cowardice defeat.

By the end of the week, word had reached the ears of King Antiochus VII Sidetes in Antioch, Syria about all the events that had taken place in his western kingdom. He was very grieved to find out about the murder of his friend and ally Shim'own Maccabim. He was also very angry that his appointed governor, long-time friend and ex-general would devise such a murderous plot against his own father-in-law to gain additional political power. Then there was the feeling of deep disappointment in Yhowchanan Hyrcanus I who did not level the city of Yriychow to avenge the murder of his father and brothers yet he could not be too mad at him because the king knew how much Yhowchanan loved his mother and her suffering tore deeply at his heart. Regardless of his feelings and emotions at the time, he had to take strong action against both parties or else the Roman Republic would take away his throne and kingdom because of its unrest. Quick and strong action would be required to hold the throne in Antioch, Syria. By nightfall King Antiochus VII Sidetes had mustered up one-hundred and forty-three thousand men as an army to straighten out this potential political catastrophe. At the breaking of the pre-dawn light the next morning they would begin their march towards the strong city of Yriychow (Jericho).

It would take a six-day march to cover the nearly three-hundred miles from Antioch, Syria southeast towards the strong city of Yriychow. King Antiochus VII Sidetes would not push his troops because they had to be fresh to do battle at sunrise of the fifth day. They traveled through Galilee and in the Plain of Esdraelon the army split with half taking the road east to the city of Scythopolis in the territory of Decapolis and then would follow the Yardan (Jordan) River south and attack Yriychow (Jericho) from the north. The other continued south through the territory of Samaria and would cross the hills between the cities of Beyth'el (Bethel) and Ramah approaching Yriychow from the heights of the mountains west of the strong city. This left the only escape available for Ptolomee, son of Abubus to go south to the Wilderness of Yhuwdah where he would face King Herod Atticus of Idumea (Edom) leaving him trapped by the Dead Sea. When the northern army of King Antiochus VII approached the city of Scythopolis, a spy from Yriychow was staying at the local Inn and immediately left at gallop speed to warn Ptolomee. The army would still be an eight-hour march away yet the speedy horse could make it in four hours giving Ptolomee a four to five hour advantage to escape if he chose not to fight.

What the rider did not know was that it was a mere deception as the smaller northern army rested an entire day before approaching the city of Scythopolis allowing the main force of the army to arrive hidden in the hills west of Yriychow eighteen-hours before word could reach Ptolomee. Also, news would reach the great city of Yruwshalaim one day prior to attacking the city of Yriychow but King Antiochus VII Sedetes knew that the distraught Yhowchanan Hyrcanus I Maccabim would not leave the city and that he would choose to do battle if the crown of Antioch, Syria tried once again to take away the independence of the Hebrew people. Even at that, the great city of Yruwshalaim would only have two days to prepare for the inevitable onslaught of destruction.

The deceptive ploy of Antiochus VII Sedetes worked as Ptolomee knew he was trapped from the north so he fled the strong city of Yriychow (Jericho) south to the wilderness where the main force of Antiochus VII Sedetes ran him down and killed him before he and his fleeing army could reach Ideumea (Edom). Antiochus VII Sedetes and his main army joined with the northern army who were waiting at the strong city of Yriychow. It was beginning to get dark, so Antiochus decided to remain in Yriychow and then at pre-dawn light begin the invasion of the territory of Yhuwdah (Judea) and to destroy the great city of Yruwshalaim to punish his long time ally Yhowchanan Hyrcanus I Maccabim for being a coward. The next morning after a fast-paced march of three hours the army of one-hundred and forty-three thousand found itself on the outskirt of the great city of Yruwshalaim. However, before King Antiochus VII Sedetes would give the signal for an all out siege on the city, he summoned Yhowchanan Hyrcanus I to parlay with him in his royal tent. The royal entourage of the Hebrew leader arrived in the midst of the massive Grecian-Syrian army and was led to the tent of the king.

When he arrived through the open flap of the pure white tent covered with golden lined scallops surrounding the top of the tent, Antiochus VII Sedetes said in a serious and commanding voice, "Sit down young Hyrcanus we have serious business to discuss or you and your people will lose more innocent lives." Yhowchanan obeyed the king and gave him a quick nod as if he understood. Then the king continued, "Yhowchanan Hyrcanus I *ben* (son of) Shim'own Maccabim, it is only out of the respect and honor of your slain father that I offer a proposal to you before I destroy your city and your people. However, first I want to inform you that your murderous brother-in-law, Ptolomee, son of Abubus and his army has been executed in the Wilderness of Yhuwdah to avenge the blood of your entire family. I will not allow one hint of upheaval in my kingdom to reach the ears of the Roman Republic and portray that I have lost control. As you know, all Rome requires of us is that our territories remain in peace. Therefore, before I present my proposal I am going to give you some advice that your father would have given you if he was alive."

"What good did it do for you to turn tail and run like a coward with your superior army from Yriychow except to shorten the suffering of your mother but it did not save her life did it? How much more suffering do you think she and your sister endured after your cowardice retreat? You were entrusted by your father with a territory of people to lead and protect. As a leader you can't allow your emotions and feelings on a battlefield to cloud over the purpose of the battle in the first place. You went to Yriychow to avenge the death of your father and brothers knowing full well that there was a very slim chance of saving your mother and sister. You failed to honor your dead father and dishonored your mother and sister, leaving them to be sacrificial lambs of shame. The sacrifice of *One Lamb* in *The Dawning* light for the good of many people should have been your decision."

"You forced me and my men at my expense to bring honor to your dead father and brothers and to avenge the horrific executions of your beloved mother and beautiful sister. Now you must pay for the great expense that has come out of my treasury to fulfill your duties to uphold your family's honor. There is rumor that Parthia (Persia, modern Iran) is once raising its head towards my throne and I can't be distracted by such an expense or constant turmoil because of the cowardice of a territory's leader. You will either pay today with your blood and the innocent blood of your people, the Hebrews, or you will unconditionally accept my proposal."

"Here is my masterful proposal that could save your life, continue the Hasmonean leadership in the territory of Yhuwdah, and preserve the great city of Yruwshalaim and the worship of the Hebrew people:

First, since you are a yellow-bellied coward and failed to lead your people with wisdom, you shall be nothing more than a mere puppet and pawn for my throne. Second, since I had to defend the honor of your family, you must pay me three-thousand talents prior to me leaving this battlefield today. Third, you and the Hebrew people shall break down all the walls of the great city of Yruwshalaim before my commanders will leave this battlefield with their armies. Fourth, the Hebrew people in the territory of Yhuwdah (Judea) shall once again pay taxes to my treasury. Fifth, you shall dissolve the agreement with Rome as being a semi-independent nation from the rule of my throne in Antioch, Syria and your people shall exist as part of Grecian-Syria and no longer a separate nation. Sixth and finally, you and your army will assist me in defending and conquering the territory of Parthia (Iran) with the expenses for your army coming out of your own treasuries."

King Antiochus VII Sedetes made a long pause and studied the countenance of Yhowchanan Hyrcanus I and then slammed his fist into his hand and said, "What is your decision, death or degradation? I need your answer now! My troops do not have all day to wait." Yhowchanan Hyrcanus I slowly raised up to his feet and with nerves of steel and the blood of generations of Maccabim flowing through his veins clearly and boldly stated, "Old friend and ally, before I give you my final answer, just know that I have learned a valuable lesson over this past week. Also, know this in your heart that I will never ever make that mistake again. My decision is based upon what my Grandfather Matityahu Maccabim would do in this situation and not because of your condescending terms of what you call a proposal. You know very well that I come from a long line of powerful and proud *gammedim*, warriors, and I am not afraid to die here or on the battlefield. Therefore, I want to make it perfectly clear that under no certain terms will I accept any proposal from anyone in degradation! I will be glad to meet your terms in honor as paying a debt to a good friend for taking care of my family's business while I was momentarily distraught and did not have my wits about me. Therefore, the acceptance of this proposal is not for me to make but for you to accept my payment of gratitude as a long-time friend. I need your answer immediately as I have a lot to do for an old friend of mine." With a slight smile, Yhowchana Hyrcanus I turned and started to walk out of the tent when he heard a voice from behind him say, "I accept your payment old friend. Now, may peace keep both of us safe. My army will stand down and I will await for your gifts before sunset this eve." So, in 134 B.C. the territory of Yhuwdah once again became under the control of the throne in Antioch, Syria but the people were free to worship Yahuah according to the Law and Commandments.

Within a new moon (month) all terms of the proposal had been met so the vast army of King Antiochus VII Sedetes headed back home in late spring, three-hundred miles north to Antioch, Syria. However, by early summer all was not well in the great city of Yruwshalaim. The political party of the *Chaciydim*, Hasidim began arguing among themselves over religious and political matters. The majority of them supported the actions of Yhowchanan Hyrcanus I in meeting the terms of King Antiochus VII Sedetes while a minority detested it and called Yhowchanan a traitor because he robbed the tomb of King David to pay the demanded three-thousand talents of silver. They called it 'blood-money' and interrupted Yhowchanan's actions by religious law as defiling the temple by hiring a 'mercenary' with sacred funds to do what he should have done himself on the battlefield at the city of Yriychow (Jericho).

This heated bickering that hot summer over the interpretation of Yhowchanan's actions split the *Chaciydim*, Hasidim into three political religious parties. The majority called themselves **Pharisees** and supported Yhowchanan Hyrcanus I. The scribes were not really interested in political or military power. They simply sought to impose strict orthodox religious purity, ridged outward observance of the Law and were the most influential of the three sects. A second group from the Hasidim, the **Essenes** chose to live a somewhat monastic existence. Therefore, they lived a quiet, withdrawn life near the Dead Sea and it was this group of pious, committed Hebrews who would become responsible for producing the now famous *Dead Sea Scrolls*. A third party, the **Sadducees** were more interested in political power and who favored a more Hellenistic (Greek) way of life. They believed one could successfully compromise with the Hellene (Greek) teachings and way of life and still remain loyal to Yahuah. They objected to the strictness and legalistic mindset of the Pharisees, did not believe in the Oral Law or resurrection of the dead and believed that the control of the religious affairs of the common people should reside only in the hands of the *kohen*, priests. They loved to collaborate with the ruling powers to obtain special favor over the other two religious factions and were considered the elite upper class.

9

Satan's evil minions now had spread their demonic poison into the religious organization of the Hebrew people. They were no longer unified with one mind dedicated to fellowship with Yahuah Yahusha. The summer of 134 B.C. experienced more heat from the hatred between these three political-religious factions than the actual temperature of the air. Yowchanan Hyrcanus I was not able to squelch this growing ember because he could not regain the respect of the smaller minority party of the Sadducees. By mid-summer so much hate and dissention existed between the Pharisees and the Sadducees that the third party of the Essenes left the great city of Yruwshalaim and moved twenty miles to the east to the caves of the Dead Sea at a settlement called Khirbet Qumran. They were the only religious leaders who would not allow themselves to be stung by the poisonous tails of the bestial serpents. They wanted to be left alone dedicated to Yahuah Yahusha to be *checed*, pious, and *tsadaq*, righteous. The Essenes continued to be a pre-dawn light in the east as the sun would rise over the hills of Yhuwdah (Judea). However, the minions of Satan made sure that any pre-dawn light would have to peep through dark storm clouds of wicked demise leading to the death and destruction of man's fellowship with Yahuah Yahusha.

Yhowchanan Hyrcanus I sat on a marble bench facing the largest fountain in the beautiful garden of the Hasmonean Palace. The constant gentle cascading water took his thoughts deep within his soul. The aromatic aromas of roses, lavender and lilacs soothed his troubled mind. The cool of the shaded breeze softly combed and twisted through his hair as his mother used to do with her long gentle fingers. Tears began to well up in his eyes and slowly trickle down his cheeks into his youthful beard as he yearned to tell his mother how much he loved her and was sorry to disappoint her. Then he was startled as he felt a sudden taping on his ankle. It was old Hagar trying to get his attention with her now required walking stick. The tragedy of Shim'own Maccabim and his entire family took a major toll on the already aged woman. "Sorry, I did not see you approach," Yhowchanan said to Hagar. "I know young master, it is hard not to be ambushed when you are a million miles away, eh?" in a nurturing voice replied Hagar.

Then the emotions of Yhowchanan Hyrcanus I exploded and he released them upon faithful Hagar, "Oh Hagar, I have made such a mess of things. I have dishonored the Maccabim name, disappointed my mother in her last moments on earth, sold my family and the Hebrew people back to slavery of Antioch, Syria and now the *Chaciydim,* Hasidim have split apart hating each other and some even moving away from this great city all because they have lost *chacuwth,* confidence, in me. My beautiful wife and two young sons are in the town of Gazara far away from this mess but I even sold that city to the control of the throne in Antioch. Oh how I miss the playful giggles of my two sons." Yhowchanan sobbed uncontrollably placing his hands over his face as his shoulders heaved up and down. Old Hagar placed her hand on top of his head and said, "Young master being a leader is a heavy burden and must not be shared alone. Old Hagar is tired and can't help because soon I will sleep with my ancestors who have gone before me. However, today your faithful servant has a surprise for you to help lift your spirits."

At that moment the lattice garden gate burst open and from

under the arched arbor covered with bright yellow and pink climbing roses came the pattering of little feet screaming with glee, "*Ab, ab, father father!*" Towards the marble bench ran six-year old Yhuwdah (Judas) Hyrcanus Maccabim who was called by his Hellene (Greek) name of Aristobulus I, meaning 'good counselor', and right on his heels was his four-year old brother called Antigonus, which has a Greek meaning of 'worthy of father'. They leapt wildly into the now open arms of Yhowchanan Hyrcanus I kissing his cheeks as he held them tight to his bosom. After seeing the joyful family reunion, old Hagar began to return to her servant quarters when she heard a quivering voice from behind her saying, "Thank you faithful one. You always knew how to mend my broken heart." As she closed the door which led to her quarters, she briefly watched Hyrcanus fall to the ground and wrestle with his two small opponents. Their small infectious giggles brought much needed laughter back into the Maccabim house.

Four years flew by fast as Yhowchanan Hyrcanus I enjoyed having his wife and especially his two little sons near him. Faithful Hagar, his mother's maidservant passed away in the early winter of 134 B.C. shortly after the arrival of his wife and the two sons that he loved so much. Yhowchanan took advantage of the peace in the territory of Yhuwdah (Judea) and the calm of the internal political-religious fighting between the Pharisees and the Sadducees. Yhowchanan spent many nights walking through the palace gardens with his beautiful wife holding hands and standing under the pure light of the moon embracing and caressing each other. Their love for each other deepened so much that one could not be seen without the other. He doted over his two sons something terribly spending a great amount of time with them on a daily basis. He made sure that they had religious training from the Pharisees which pleased this party and gratified the Sadducees by the two boys receiving their secular educational training from Hellene (Greek) teachers. Their military training and strategies were composed of learning by heart the accolades and war stories of their deceased great-grandfather Matityahu Maccabim and their great uncles Yhuwdah (Judas) "the Hammer" and Yhownathan (Jonathan) "the Diplomat".

Then in the early spring of 130 B.C. came the dreaded day Yhowchanan Hyrcanus I had hoped would never come. A royal messenger sent from the throne of Atiochus VII Sedetes in the city of Antioch, Syria delivered a parchment to Yhowchanan. After the rider handed the parchment to Yhowchanan, he turned to head back down the dusty road three-hundred miles to Syria. Yhowchanan Hyrcanus I stood there frozen for a moment holding the parchment down to his side as he watched the rider disappear from his sight down the cobbled stone street. Then he felt the hand of his wife upon his left shoulder and heard her mutter softly in a shaky whisper, "No, not now." He turned and faced his wife looking into her deep brown eyes which were beginning to moisten. He embraced her and held her to his bosom tightly and said, "Let me just hold you in this moment before I read this official document." After a long embrace, he gave her a kiss on her olive-colored forehead, released her and began to read the open parchment out loud, "*I, King Antiochus VII Sedetes now demand that you fulfill your last obligation of the 'gift' to an 'old friend'. You and an army of forty-five thousand men will meet me in Antioch, Syria to prepare for war against Parthia* (Persia-modern Iran) *in one month. Your willing participation in this endeavor is much appreciated. Consider your father's honor of the Maccabim name fulfilled after the impending victory in Parthia. Signed, your Old Friend Antiochus VII.*" Yhowchanan began gathering his army and chose the fan-maker, who was famous for his ostrich feathered fans that hung over many wealthy dining areas, Ashar'Shamar (Edward) Aer as his armor bearer. The name of Ashar'Shamar means 'rich guard' and the last name of Aer means 'breath'. This was a fitting name for an armor bearer meaning 'rich guard of breath'. Then the last week of the month, Yhowchanan Hyrcanus I with his armor bearer Ashar'Shamar Aer and the army of forty-five thousand men departed and marched to Antioch, Syria.

While Yhowchanan (John) Hyrcanus I was absent from the great city of Yruwshalaim over the next two years, he had lost the support of the Yhuwdiy (Jews) in various cultural sectors. Those powerful in the great city of Yruwshalaim and the countryside Yhuwdiy along with the religious leadership doubted the future of Yhuwdah (Judea) under the rule of Yhowchanan Hyrcaus I. Most of the irritation came because of the loss of governmental funds for a war that was not theirs and loss of Yhuwdiy life in battle. The real rub came in the fact that taxation for Antioch, Syria continued to burden the Hebrew people during the recent drought. Their men were required to risk their lives and shed their blood for the very throne that imposed financial hardship on the lives of the Hebrews. While Yhowchanan was absent from his throne the Pharisees and the Sadducees formed a ruling religious body of seventy Rabbi's dominated by the Pharisees called the Sanhedrin

Then Yhowchanan Hyrcanus I was met with fortune in the early spring of 128 B.C. when the two nations claimed victory in Parthia and King Antiochus VII Sedetes was killed in battle. The Grecian-Syrian army returned to Antioch, Syria with General Antiochus VIII Gryphos the son of Demetrius II Nicator and brother to Antiochus VII Sedetes. He quickly declared himself king and respected Yhowchanan Hyrcanus I promising to remain at peace with him and the Hebrew people. Therefore, Yhowchanan returned back to the territory of

Yhuwdah (Judea) victorious and with thirty-seven thousand Hebrew *gammedim*, warriors, losing only eight-thousand on the battlefield. As they were a distance from the great city of Yruwshalaim they could hear the sounding of the *showphars*, the curved ram horn trumpets sounding the victory blasts. When they got close to the ruins of what used to be the city walls, the celebratory shouts and music could be heard plainly. Yhowchanan nudged his stallion in the side to a gentle gallop as he climbed the cobblestone street towards the Hasmonean Palace. A much welcomed sight filled his eyes as he saw his two sons now twelve and ten years old, running in front of their mother to meet him. They were skipping and screaming, "*ab teshuw'ah*, father is delivered free and safe." He quickly dismounted his stallion and pulled his two growing sons into his bosom. He thought, *my how they have grown the past two years.* Then his wife joined in the family hug and they just stood there in the middle of the cobblestone street embraced in a tight huddle. The dissention that had been in the air prior to his arrival seemed to evaporate as the people watched and became a witness to the strong bond of love that his family held dearly for each other.

Later that spring in 128 B.C. Yhowchanan Hyrcanus I sent a delegation to Rome to once again speak to the Roman Senate of the young Roman Republic. The Senate reaffirmed their support for the Hebrew people in the territory of Yhuwdah (Judea) and recognized Hasmonean rule. They also, once again gave them semi-independence but not total independence from the throne in Antioch, Syria. Also, that year Yhowchanan ceased paying tribute taxes to the throne of Antioch, Syria and began rebuilding the strong walls of the great city of Yruwshalaim. His popularity among the Yhuwdiy (Jews) during this new period of peace soared as he once again became a favored son as finally being regarded as of the Maccabim family. Over the next fifteen years of total peace, Yowchanan Hyrcanus I produced three more sons, yet he truly only loved his two oldest. Even though he was Hebrew royalty he acted and governed as a common citizen. His two oldest children, however, were an entirely different matter! Being raised in a luxurious palace, Yhuwdah Aristobulus I and Antigonus regarded themselves as Aristocrats superior to other people. Their schooling was more in the Greek than the Hebrew areas of study, and they came to regard the Pharisees with outright loathing. Although their father was a devout Pharisee, they sided more with the Hellenistic Sadducees.

It is now early spring 113 B.C. and trouble once again began brewing with the throne of Antioch, Syria. Antiochus VIII Gryphus was challenged by his nephew Antiochus IX Cyzicenus, son of Antiochus VII Sidetes. The challenge didn't last long and Antiochus VIII Gryphus remained on the throne in Antioch, Syria while Antiochus IX Cyzicenus was allowed to be king only in the city of Coele, Syria. Both kings continued to leave Yhowchanan Hyrcanus I and the territory of Yhuwdah alone and at peace. The Hebrew people were not subject to either king in Syria. Yhowchanan Hyrcanus I saw a window of opportunity and appointed his sons Aristobulus I now twenty-seven years old and Antigonus now twenty-five years old as commanding generals of the entire Hebrew army. It was this year that the Hasmonean Dynasty expanded its territory and the two young generals captured the territories of Samaria and Galilee to the north and Idumea (Edom) to the south. They even killed King Herod Atticus of Idumea. Yhowchanan decreed that the new territories that were added to his kingdom of Yhuwdah (Judea) must be circumcised and follow only the Law and Commandments of Yahuah Yahusha.

The two young generals returned home to the great city of

Yruwshalaim in the very late fall of 113 B.C. Their father brimming with pride threw a huge welcome-home-victory party. The entire Sanhedrin of Pharisee and Sadducee rabbi's were invited with essentially the entire region surrounding the great city of Yruwshalaim. Not only were they going to celebrate the young generals' recent victories but Yhowchanan Hyrcanus I Maccabim was going to rededicate the rebuilt walls now providing protection to the great city. These two events were important to Hebrew history but would not compare in importance or significance in history of a historical accidental meeting that occurred during this celebration. After the rededication of the rebuilt walls held in the Bezetha District in front of the North Wall, the procession of celebration traveled to the Upper City towards the Hasmonean Palace. Here, General Aristobulus I and General Antigonus were to be honored by their father with much pomp and fanfare. Yhowchanan Hyrcanus I called his sons to come forward to a makeshift platform with six steps so everyone could see and witness their crowning achievement. In the front row of course were members of the Sanhedrin in which one guest was permitted to accompany and sit beside them. The most important Rabbi's and leadership of the Sanhedrin were stood near the center steps leading up to the makeshift platform where Yhowchanan was already standing next to his beautiful wife. The two generals walked up the center isle towards the platform waving and greeting people in the large crowd as they made their way to the front. Just as Aristobulus I was about to step on the first step someone in the crowd yelled, "*Heydad Aristobulus I,* Hooray Aristobulus I." He tried to turn around mid-step to wave but he missed the step and fell over backwards and knocked over a young woman.

This was no ordinary young woman as she was the guest of one of the Sanhedrin. The member of the Sanhedrin just happened to be

Rabbi Setah BarYossei (Setah son of Yossei) the leading member of the Sanhedrin. His father was Yossei BarYowchanan (Yossei son of John) who was a member of the *Chaciydim*, Hasidim during the time of Matityahu Maccabim and his sons. His guest whom Aristobulus I leveled to the ground was none other than the very beautiful twenty-six year old daughter of Rabbi Setah BarYossei. Normally only men were allowed up front in honored places but because of his religious and political influence an exception was made. The daughter's full Hebrew name was Shalowm'Tsiyown Alexandra BetSetah (Peace of Zion, Alexandra daughter of Setah) meaning in Hebrew 'safety of the guiding pillar'. She later became known as Alexandra Salome or Alexandra of Jerusalem.

Antigonus quickly helped his older brother Aristobulus I up from on top of Alexandra as her father was also trying to lend a hand to this now comical event. As Aristobulus I was about to his feet another nearby Rabbi helped Rabbi Setah BarYossei get Alexandra BetSetah on her feet. Her sky blue silk dress was a wrinkled mess and the aqua-blue netted veil that covered her face was twisted sideways covering one eye. She had lost her left sandal being half-barefoot. Her multiple gold bracelets that had been on her wrists were now near her elbow. She was a wreck and Aristobulus I was deeply embarrassed with a tinge of red showing on his dark brown olive skinned face. Both young generals finally made their way to the platform and received their victorious war medallions on necklaces of linked chain of gold. Then it was time for Yhowchanan to make the victory speech.

"Hebrew brothers and sisters, honored members of the Sanhedrin and distinguished guests, I stand before you as a very proud Commander in Chief and father. Yahuah has been very *chesed*, gracious, to our nation ever since my grandfather Matityahu *HaGadowl Kohen,* the High Priest, began a revolt some fifty-four years ago in this very city. Today we uphold and defend the privilege to worship Yahuah according to His Law and Commandments. In the time of my grandfather, Yhuwdah was the size of a small fist but today my sons have enlarged it to the size of an open palm with fingers spreading out. Our territory now includes: Samaria, Galilee, Decapolis and Idumea (Edom). Today's territory is almost the size of our ancestor King David. It has not been easy and personal sacrifices from everyone have been required. Therefore, today is not just to honor my sons who led the armies this year but today belongs to everyone in this nation and great city." This brought a round of explosive applause and sharp shrills of the tongue that lasted over five minutes.

Then Yhowchanan Hyrcanus I continued, "Now I must warn my oldest son Aristobulus I, the apparent heir to my throne, that from this day forward he must choose his steps carefully and quoting King Solomon, 'Pride of a man goes before his fall." This brought a loud explosion of laughter from the large crowd. Then Yhowchanan turned and looked at the once again embarrassed face of Aristobulus I who smiled back at his teasing father. Then the royal family descended from the platform to the receiving line in the royal gardens. Those guests who were invited, left the general crowd in the courtyard and also made their way to the reception line for a large private banquet. As Rabbi Setah was shaking the hand of Yhowchanan, Yhowchanan said, "My sincere apologies for my son falling as a conquest for your daughter but they would make a good match, eh?" Rabbi Setah just grinned and quickly ushered his daughter into the banquet. Two months later the royal match had been made by the fathers. The heir apparent of the Maccabim Hasmonean Dynasty would be joined to the daughter of the leader of the Sanhedrin and Chief Pharisee, Rabbi Setah BarYossei. This union solidified the support to the throne from the party of the Pharisees who would vehemently defend any action of Yhowchanan Hyrcanus I including the giving of a large multi-story home at the far south side of the Upper City to the armor bearer of Yhowchanan Hyrcanus I, the fan-maker, Ashar'Shamar (Edward) Aer.

The evil minions of Satan could not cover up and hide the pre-dawn light of the coming Son for the next six years. However, in 105 B.C. their poison of deceitful lies, lust for power and murder began to intensify and this time it was the Hasmonean Dynasty that felt their sting. Sanhedrin leader Pharisee Rabbi Setah ben Yossei was retiring from his leadership position in the council and wanted to appoint his son Pharisee Rabbi Simeon ben Setah to take his seat. However, Pharisee Rabbi Eleazar believed that he should assume the coveted position since his family had donated the most money to get the Sanhedrin started and Simeon ben Setah was one of the youngest members of the seventy-rabbi member council. Rabbi Eleazar went to Yhowchanan Hyrcanus I and explained why his ambitions were so strong to usurp Setah's appointment of his son Simeon. Yhowchanan Hyrcanus I refused to oppose his daughter-in-law's father and brother and had Rabbi Eleazar abruptly escorted out of his presence by the Palace Guards into the cobblestone street. Since, Yhowchanan Hyrcanus I was the *HaGadowl Kohen*, High Priest, he would have to oversee the election of the Sanhedrin leadership tomorrow and if necessary to cast the deciding vote in case of a tie ballot. The rest of the day was a constant interruption of Rabbis from the Pharisees and the Sadducees just stopping by to give their best regards and their oh-by-the-way comments on who they would like to see him support in a close election.

The next morning was quite beautiful. Yhowchanan Hyrcanus I looked at the sea of blue above his head with small whiffs of white cottony clouds smattered here and there. The birds were singing their wake up calls as they chirped so happily as they sang to the rest of Yahuah Yahusha's creation. Aromas of fresh baking bread and sweet fragrances of blooming flowers teased his sense of smell. He crossed over the bridge that led from the Hasmonean Palace to the Royal Porch of the Temple entering just west of the Huldah Gate. This was the very gate that his grandfather and father escaped from after they sparked the 'Maccabim Revolt' some sixty-two years ago. In his mind he hoped that the election would proceed without much conflict so he could be home early to spend time alone with his wife in the garden this afternoon. After he passed the Court of the Gentiles and headed to the large meeting rooms above the Court of Women his dreams of a peaceful afternoon alone with his beautiful wife were shattered because he could hear heated arguing coming from inside the doors. As soon as the doorkeepers opened the doors and the council saw who was in the open doorway the room got quite except for respectful greetings as he took his seat to preside over the election. The voting procedure was simple. The casting of votes would start with the oldest members and would descend down in age to the youngest members to cast the final votes regardless of their party affiliation. Pharisee Rabbi Eleazar knew that he had to win over the older members of the Sanhedrin because the younger members though outnumbered considered themselves peers of the much younger candidate Pharisee Simeon ben Setah and strongly supported Yhowchanan Hyrcanus I as *HaGadowl Kohen*, High Priest since they knew nothing but peace in the territory for the past twenty-nine years.

When the voting was half way completed through the older members, Pharisee Rabbi Eleazar saw that the tallies were close in his favor but several Sadducees had not cast their votes yet who would probably vote for young Pharisee Rabbi Simeon making the vote to close to proceed into the younger members which was the stronghold for Rabbi Simeon. Therefore, he requested of Yhowchanan Hyrcanus I if he could make a brief comment about his vision for the Sanhedrin. The Sadducees began to hiss with resentment and the younger members groaned out loud. However, forty votes were yet to be casted so Yhowchanan allowed him to stand up and speak freely to the seventy-member council.

Pharisee Rabbi Eleazar stood to his feet and began the political discourse, "Fellow members of the Council, I take this moment to remind you that this is a pivotal point in the history of the Hebrew people. We must have strong leadership from the Sanhedrin to protect the Law and Commandments of Yahuah. This can only be accomplished if the Sanhedrin is vested with a leadership that is pure within our heritage to guide the religious affairs of our people. Before the remaining votes are cast it is important that those making their final decisions for proper leadership to lead and protect our Hebrew heritage must take into consideration of two facts. First, it should not be proper for *HaGadowl Kohen*, the High Priest, to cast the deciding vote as he has strong family ties to my opposing candidate and the outgoing leadership. This is what the Law defines as an unjust scale of measure and according to the law of Mosheh (Moses) should be cast out. Second, the leader of our kingdom should excuse himself because he is not a pure Hebrew. Many years ago, his mother, wife of our great leader Shim'own Maccabim, was kidnapped by the Hellene (Greek) Syrian leader Antiochus IV Epiphanes and was raped. Yhowchanan Hyrcanus I, was a result of that tragic event. I ask that the voting be stopped and that he step down immediately from *HaGadowl Kohen*, the High Priest."

Yhowchanan Hyrcanus I was immediately furious with the

evil insinuation about his dead mother and stood up pointing his finger at Pharisee Rabbi Eleazar screaming, "*Ragal! Ragal!* Slander, slander! I want this man thrown from this assembly and executed for this impertinent remark against my dead mother and myself. He has criminally insulted *HaGadowl Kohen*, the High Priest!" The Sadducees joined Yhowchanan shouting for the execution of Pharisee Rabbi Eleazar but the Pharisees who had the majority threw their support behind fellow Pharisee Rabbi Eleazar except for Pharisee Setah and his candidate son Pharisee Simeon. For three hours the shouting and arguing took place and a vote was taken to execute Rabbi Eleazar and it failed to pass. Then the vote was taken for a new leader in the Sanhedrin and Eleazar's plot failed as a large majority then voted for Pharisee Rabbi Simeon Bar Setah, who took over the leadership seat from his Pharisee Rabbi father, Simeon Bar Yossei. After the vote, Yhowchanan Hyrcanus I stormed out of the meeting chambers in complete rage and hurried straight home to the palace. His wife failed to console him to squelch his heated anger and late that night he called in the leading Sadducee and switched his support from the Pharisees to the Sadducees.

This event in the late autumn of 105 B.C. renewed the infighting between the two political-religious parties and Yhowchanan Hyrcanus I was too devastated about the lies and rumors that he lost the will to live. Therefore, he called his family together and stipulated in his will that his wife should assume political power as Queen and his oldest son, Aristobulus I should take over the position of *HaGadowl Kohen*, the High Priest. Early after the first of the new year of 104 B.C. in the middle of winter, Yhowchanan Hyrcanus I died. His wife was appointed Queen and his oldest son Yhuwdah (Judah) was appointed *HaGadowl Kohen*, the High Priest. Yhuwdah preferred to use his Helene (Greek) name of Aristobulus who soon decided that being *HaGadowl Kohen,* the High Priest was not enough and wanted control of the entire nation. So, he cast his mother, the Queen and his three younger brothers into prison and starved his mother to death. Then he gave himself the title of *nasi,* sheik or prince and High Priest of the Sanhedrin.

Over the next twelve months, Aristobulus I stayed in a close relationship with his brother Antigonus who took over as Chief General of the Military. The pressure of running a nation got to Aristobulus and he became dependent upon the *chemeth,* skin bottle, of wine to quiet the demons raging war in his head. When his wife, Alexandra Salome, became aware of his mental illness she began to work a wedge between the two brothers. Aristobulus I remained loyal to the Sadducees even though his wife preferred to support her brother Rabbi Simeon ben Shetah, who was a Pharisee and the leader of Sanhedrin. Queen Alexandra Salome, conspired to murder the king's brother, Antigonus but when that failed she poisoned the mind of Aristobulus I trying to convince him that Antigonus was attempting to steal the throne by force. The health of Aristobulus I declined so much that he shut himself up in one of the towers, called Strato's Tower, and secured it with armed guards in the stairway, as not to let the rumor get out to the public and the Sanhedrin push to take away his throne of monarchy.

Due to the constant insistency of his wife, Queen Alexandra Salome, he decided to get to the bottom of this disloyalty and arranged a casual meeting with his brother. King Aristobulus I told his guards if his brother came dressed casually then they let him pass but if armed to kill him instantly. When the queen found out the details of the meeting, she convinced Antigonus that the king wished to see him in his new armor which bore the insignia of the new king. Therefore when the unsuspecting Antigonus approached the stairwell in full battle armor to climb up the stairs, he was instantly attacked by the guards and was killed. Days later, in early 103 B.C. King Yhuwdah Aristobulus I Mabbabim died of internal bleeding from the dreadful disease that was eating his liver. The ugly black vulture of death once again had the blood of the Maccabim family on its long sharp talons. Was it through feeding on this family's flesh or was it going to hover in the dark clouds of wickedness on the lookout for its next prey? How about this evil Queen? Was she looking to take over the throne herself or did she have another deceitful plan up her sleeve? Was her brother the Pharisee involved with the murderous plot against General Antigonus Maccabee, the next rightful heir to the throne? How much more poison would flow through the veins of this evil Queen? What was the plan of Satan to enhance the destruction of the Hebrews?

Shortly after the death of the king, Queen Alexandra Salome let his remaining three brothers out of prison. The third oldest brother was Hezekiah ben Yhowchanan Maccabim. He was ultra-conservative and just wanted to live a quiet life so he left the great city of Yruwshalaim and moved with the Essenes twenty miles to the east to the caves of the Dead Sea at a settlement called Khirbet Qumran. The fourth oldest son of Yhowchanan Hyrcanus I Maccabim was Prince Absalom of Yhuwdah. He could see through the Queen so he too left the great city of Yruwshalaim and worked secretly to oppose the next heir to the throne of his father. The youngest son of Yhowchanan Hyrcanus I was Yownathan (Jonathan) Alexander Maccabee. He was the favorite of his mother as she affectionately called him 'Yannai' (Johnny) and his official Hellene (Greek) name was Alexander Jannaeus. However, his father Yhowchanan Hyrcanus I had always despised him.

Just as the vulture of death had cleared the area the black demonic serpents of Satan swooped down upon the great city of Yruwshalaim and headed straight to the Hasmonean Palace. Was the Queen their target again? Was she going to murder twenty-two year old Alexander Jannaeus? The black slender tails of the evil minion serpents were poised to sting as Alexander Jannaeus walked out the cell of the royal prison. The first person to meet him was Queen Alexandra Salome who gave him a kiss on the cheek. At that very moment two black spiritual forces attacked Alexander Jannaeus driving their stingers of their tails deep into his heart, which were dripping with poison from the evil black cauldron of Satan. Where were the *tsadaq*, righteous, to save the Hebrews? Why didn't the *checed*, pious, come to the rescue of Abraham's children?

King David's great city Yruwshalaim (Jerusalem) was a complete disaster spiritually. The power of the throne was in the hands of a Queen who was more concerned with royal court intrigue than with enforcing the Law and Commandments of Yahuah. The spiritual leadership was divided, bickering and in a power struggle against each other to subject the decisions of a seventy member council called the Sanhedrin. The rabbi's were no longer interested in their lawful duties to the temple but rather forcing their interpretations of the Law upon the opposing party and the worshipping Hebrew people. Tired of the religious leadership's bickering and infighting, the Hebrew people became lax in their worship and their fellowship with Yahuah waned.

Outside of the Hasmonean Palace in the distant land of Mitsrayim (Egypt) six-year old Boethus ben Ananelus was beginning his priestly training by his father Ananelus ben Ananias and his grandfather Ananias ben Onais V. He was a very bright Hebrew boy. At the age of three he already knew the *otiyot yehsod*, alphabet and could name the first six generations of Abraham. His great-grandfather, Onais

V, a leading member of the *Chaciydim*, Hasidim escaped from the great city of Yruwshalaim when Viceroy Lysias under orders from King Antiochus IV Epiphanes, to execute him after the start of the Maccabim Revolt had started. Rabbi Onais V went to Leontopolis, Mitsrayim (Egypt) and started a temple there for the Hebrew-Egyptian people in 159 B.C. Rabbi Onais V was good friends of King Herod Atticus of Idumea (Edom) whom the sons of Yhowchanan Hyrcanus I Maccabim killed when they added the territory of Idumea (Edom) to Yhuwdah (Judea). Now in 103 B.C. his great-grandson Boethus was being trained to be a Sadducee Rabbi. It was the hope and dream of his grandfather, Rabbi Ananias that one day Boethus would be able to sit on the council of the Sanhedrin in the great city of Yruwshalaim representing the division of the Sadducees. Was the black billowing smoke of the wicked cauldron of Satan blowing over Mitsrayim (Egypt) aimed at this cute, curly brown-haired and brown eyed little six-year old boy? How could this little boy affect the outcome of the Hebrew people and ultimately mankind so far away from the great city of Yruwshalaim? No matter how small or how far away the demonic eerie hissing began to invade the little boy's ears and mind.

Across the hot and dry blowing sands of the desert of Mitsrayim (Egypt) back in the great city of Yruwshalaim (Jerusalem) another event took place in 103 B.C. At the far south end of the Upper City in the large three-story house belonging to Ashar'Shamar Aer (Edward Ayers) stood a very proud father holding a new-born baby boy who was to be named on the eighth day after he was circumcised. He was a scrapping baby and strongly commanded to be fed or rocked to sleep. There was no doubt who was giving the final orders in this household. It was the seven pound three ounce bundle of joy in his father's arms. After being scolded by the midwife who had just finished cleaning up and attending to his wife, Ashar'Shamar gave the screaming bundle to the midwife who took the baby back to his mother to nurse. Then Ashar'Shamar went to the Temple to find Pharisee Rabbi Simeon ben Shetah to schedule the little *ben's muwlah*, sons's circumcision. For the next seven days Ashar'Shamar was badgered by relatives and the nosy gossips from the market trying to find out the name of his baby boy even though they knew full well that he could not give out the name.

The eighth day finally came and it was beautiful. The pre-dawn light seemed to have a little extra color in the horizon as the sun rose in the bright blue sky shining its warm rays upon the bustling great city of Yruwshalaim. At the south end of this bustling city in the Upper City the *Kohen*, priest was on his way to the house of Ashar'Shamar Aer. When he arrived he had to wade his way through a throng of relatives and well-wishers of the eight-day old guest of honor. It was time to begin the *brit milah*, covenant of circumcision and the *mohel*, circumciser, took the sharp flint stone and preformed the *muwlah*, circumcision, as the *Gadawl Kohen*, High Priest, Pharisee Rabbi Simeon ben Shetah held the naked little boy. Then Pharisee Rabbi Simeon ben Shetah handed the baby to his father, Ashar'Shamar who was grinning from ear-to-ear, and said, "*Yahuah barak ben Ashar'Shamar Aer*, Yahweh bless the son of Ashar'Shamar Aer." Ashar'Shamar had to clear a little tear of joy that had formed in the corners of his eyes, held the baby boy above his head towards the crowd, cleared his throat and said with such joy and happiness, "Little baby you are my *ben*, son, and I am your *ab*, father. Today I dedicate you to Yahuah our Great Eternal Father. I give you a name to follow with all your heart His Law and Commandments. You shall be called Melek'Beyth (Henry) Aer (Ayers) ben Ashar'Shamar, King of the Home son of Ashar'Shamar." The crowd erupted in tremendous applause and sharp shrills of the tongue in agreement.

10

When Aristobulus I Maccabim died in 103 B.C., his thirty-seven year old widow married his baby brother who at this time was twenty-two years old. Alexander Yownathan Maccabim took over the throne with Alexandra Salome as his Queen and gave himself the name of Alexander Jannaeus. Alexander was a Sadducee and a lover of the Greek way of life. The poison of the dark bestial minions of Satan ran full in his veins as he was uncouth, a drunk, and guilty of all manner of scandalous behavior. The Hebrew people who were still faithful to Yahuah and to the Law and Commandments absolutely hated him. One of his first official acts as King of Yhuwdah (Judea) was to appoint Herod Antipas as governor of Idumea (Edom). It was the brother of Alexander, Aristobulus I Maccabim who had killed the father of Herod Antipas, the wicked Helene (Greek) loving King Herod Atticus.

King Alexander Jannaeus being a Sadducee constantly fought and was in turmoil with the majority party of the Queen's brother Pharisee Rabbi Simon ben Shetah. Queen Alexandra Salome being fifteen years older than her husband the king, constantly wielded her power with him inciting him to continually be expanding the kingdom of their throne. The next nine years were full of battles and land acquisition with the ambition of King Alexander Jannaeus to have a territory as big as King David of ancient times. Their marriage produced two boys. The oldest was Hyrcanus II named for the king's father and the youngest was Aristobulus II named for the king's oldest brother. Hyrcanus II was favored by his mother thus was brought up leaning towards the political party of the Pharisees but Aristobulus II was favored by his father and was brought up leaning towards the political party of the Sadducees. This created a childhood dissention between the two brothers as they grew up. As children you could always here Hyrcanus II chide Aristobulus II with, "You are nothing but a Sadducee because you are always sad-you-see." Then younger Aristobulus II took his best shot with, "You are nothing but a Pharisee because you are never fair-you-see." Their parents thought it was quite comical but the two boys continued to allow this difference to grow into hatred as their ages got older.

In the year of 94 B.C., at Sukkot, the Biblical Feast of Tabernacles, King Alexander Jannaeus who was also *Gadowl Kohen*, was officiating in the Temple during the feast. Then he allowed his hatred and discontent for the Pharisees go too far and performed an act that displayed his contempt for their strict, legalistic observance of the letter of the Law and Commandments. In front of all the people, during this holy occasion, he poured out the water offering at his own feet rather than upon the altar of Yahuah as prescribed by Law. Thus, he presented himself to be the god of the Hebrew people. The people in the Temple began screaming, "*Cheneph! Cheneph!* religiously soiled, religiously soiled!" Then those in the crowd loyal to the Pharisees began throwing fruit at King Alexander producing the effect that he wanted. The sky above turned black with churning clouds as the Vulture of Death began circling and extended his long sharp blood-thirsty talons. Then all at once it began a nosedive into the courtyard of the Temple screeching eerie screams. King Alexander plotted how he could create a revolt among the Hebrews loyal to the majority party of the Pharisees thus allowing his mercenary army to attack the unarmed worshipers.

King Alexander gave the signal and his band of criminals massacred six-thousand innocent Hebrew worshippers leaving their flesh strung out in the courtyard.

As a result of this atrocity against Yauaeh and the Hebrew people, a civil war broke out in the land of Yhuwdah (Judea). The Pharisees raised an army of rebels led by Prince Absalom Maccabim of Yhuwdah and for the next six years fiercely fought against his brother King Alexander Jannaeus and his Sadducee forces. At the end of six years and fifty-thousand men of Yhuwdah (Judea) dead in 88 B.C., Prince Absalom Maccabim and the Pharisees managed to defeat King Alexander Jannaeus. The evil minions of Satan began swirling in the clouds after their defeat filling the air with the mind-clouding toxins from the steam coming out of their flaring nostrils. Then all of a sudden the Pharisees made a serious error in judgment. They convinced Prince Absalom Maccabim of Yhuwdah that his brother, the defeated King Alexander Jannaeus and his followers had been punished enough and that they had probably "learned their lesson" and allowed him to retake the throne as king of the territory of Yhuwdah. This pleased the Sadducee Rabbi's and held a quick council with King Alexander.

After King Alexander Jannaeus sat once again on the throne, he immediately ordered a lavish banquet to be held in appreciation of allowing him to regain the throne and invited his brother Prince Absalom of Yhuwdah and all the Pharisees and their families to attend. It was to be in their honor! Prince Absalom of Yhuwdah questioned the Pharisees reminding them this sure seemed the same as what had happened to his grandfather Shim'own Maccabim at the invitation of Governor Ptolomee, son of Abubus. The Pharisees called him paranoid and assumed that his motive of bringing this incident up was of a jealousy to gain the throne himself. Therefore,

Prince Absalom of Yhuwdah gave in and agreed to attend with the support of the Pharisees.

Over eight-hundred leading Pharisees and their families assembled to enjoy the feast. As they reclined on the courtyard of the Hasmonean Palace, King Alexander Jannaeus ordered his soldiers to take them all captive and while he and his concubines reclined on their royal couches and got drunk he had all eight-hundred Pharisees crucified in front of him beginning with his brother Prince Absalom Maccabim of Yhuwdah. As the Pharisees hung dying on their crosses, their wives and children of these dying men were tortured and slaughtered in their presence. The horrific Vulture of Death once again swooped down upon the great city of Yruwshalaim and filled his stomach with the flesh of the Maccabim family and the Hebrew people. As his long blood-thirsty talons and sharp beak tore at the dying faithful of Yahuah Yahusha the evil minion serpents roared with hideous eerie laughter. From that evil black cauldron of Satan belched billowing thick smoke from the depths of Hell and Death and Hades lead a demonic victory cry of hissing and howling. The faithful Hebrews in the territory heard about this barbaric act and fled to the wilderness and lived in the caves with the monastic Essenes.

King Alexander Jannaeus did not have to be concerned about the possibility of a strong reprisal from the Roman Republic due to political instability in Rome at that time. The wicked minions of darkness were pleasing their dark lord because they were also at work in Rome causing a Civil Social War between the Italian allies and the Latin allies in 88 B.C. Thus Rome was chiefly concerned with a tumultuous domestic perdicament not the hideous massacre of Hebrew people in a far away territory of Yhuwdah (Judea). The Roman Civil War began because Senator Marcus Livius Drusus presented reforms to the Senate that would have granted the Roman

Italian allies Roman citizenship. This would have given them a greater say in the external policy of the Roman Republic such as when the alliance would go to war and how they would divide the plunder. However, Senator Drusus was assassinated and most of his reforms addressing these grievances were declared invalid by the Senate. This angered the Roman allies greatly and most of them allied with one another against Rome. Dictator Lucius Cornelius Sulla crushed the revolt by the Italian allies and called upon a young statesman by the name of Julius Caesar to help solidify the thirty-five tribes of Rome.

Just who was this young Julius Caesar and why were Satan's wicked minions following him so closely? What did he have to do with the Hebrew people and the Maccabim family? What connections did he have with the Sanhedrin and did he support the Pharisees or the Sadducees? Was he to have an effect on the Temple in Egypt now under the control of Sadducee Rabbi Ananelus? Why was Satan sending legions of wicked demonic beasts to attack the Roman Republic and its governmental officials in the Roman Senate? Was the pre-dawn light about to be overshadowed with dark storm clouds of wickedness? Was mankind about to fall forever into the lordship of the dark lord? Once again from the depth of Hell, Death and Hades roared with a raucous demonic victory cry of hissing and eerie howling as the death and destruction of fellowship between Yahuah Yahusha and mankind began to wane and grow dim. The faithful knew that this just could not be the end but where was that rotating sword of light from Yahuah Yahusha? How much darker could the world of man get?

Julius Caesar was born in 100 B.C. to Gaius Julius Caesar III and wife, Aurelia Cotta. His father was the governor of the province of Asia (Turkey) and his mother came from an influential Latin family who were members of the Roman Senate. His father's sister Julia, married Gaius Marius the most powerful Senator on the Council. His family was among the most powerful elite aristocrats in the Roman Republic. His father died suddenly in 85 B.C. leaving fifteen-year old Julius Caesar as head of the family. Dictator Lucius Cornelius Sulla, in 84 B.C. appointed Julius Caesar as the new *Flamen Dialis,* high priest of Jupiter, meaning Sky-god Father. The main function of the high priest was to protect the Roman gods especially Jupiter from being overthrown by gods of foreign territories and Imperial Rome only held Jupiter as the chief god. He also had to oversee all the sacrifices made to this satanic god to insure military victory over the opponents of Rome.

One of the requirements of the *Flamen Dialis*, high priest of Jupiter, was to be married to a daughter of an elite family of ancient Rome. This presented a problem to the fifteen-year old Julius Caesar as he had been engaged since boyhood to a daughter of a *plebeian*, a free commoner that was a land-owning Roman citizen. Therefore, he broke off the engagement and married the eleven-year old Cornelia, the daughter of Lucius Cornelius Cinna, president of the Roman Senate. However, they actually would not come together for four more years, in 81 B.C. Lucius Cornelius Cinna and the uncle of Julius Caesar opposed the constant warring campaigns of Dictator Lucius Cornelius Sulla. Therefore, when Dictator Lucius Cornelius Sulla returned home to Rome later that year, he busied himself executing all his political enemies. This made Julius Caesar an easy target since he was the son-in-law of Senator Cinna and the nephew of Senator Marius. Therefore, Dictator Sulla stripped Julius Caesar of his inheritance, his wife's dowry, his priesthood and ordered him to divorce Cornelia. He refused to divorce Cornelia and was forced to go into hiding, fearing for his life. Eventually the threat against him by Dictator Sulla was lifted because of the interventions of his mother's family, who supported Dictator Sulla. Then Julius Caesar joined the military and left Rome for a campaign in Spain

At this time in 88 B.C. another prominent Roman was being injected with the poisonous venom of the wicked beasts. While they were attacking Julius Caesar and the Roman Republic demonic spiritual forces were also focused on a young Roman named Gnaeus Pompeius Magnus, called Pompey. He was born in the Italian town of Picenum on September 29, 106 B.C. His father Gnaeus Pompeius Strabo was a very wealthy landowner and a military general for Dictator Lucius Cornelius Sulla during his battle with Gaius Marius, the uncle of Julius Caesar for control of Rome. At the age of eighteen Pompey began his military career with his father, the general in 88 B.C. Then in 86 B.C. his father General Gnaeus Pompeius Strabo was struck by lightning on the battlefield. Therefore, Dictator Sulla appointed Pompey, the twenty-year old son of the general as Commanding General of the Sulla forces. Thus, his father's vast estates, political leanings and the loyalty of his troops became his inheritance. When Pompey returned to Rome he was prosecuted for misappropriation of the plunder. However, his quick marriage to the judge's daughter Antistia secured a rapid acquittal. Then in 83.B.C. three years later, when he returned home from a military campaign of the Mithridatic War Dictator Lucius Cornelius Sulla insisted that he marry his step-daughter because he was impressed by Pompey's self-confident military performance. Her name was Aemilia Scaura and was already married and pregnant. She divorced her husband and Pompey divorced his first wife, Antistia and married Sulla's step-daughter to confirm his loyalty and to boost his military career with Dictator Sulla. Aemilia died in childbirth soon after the marriage along with the baby.

The dark cloud of wicked demonic beasts turned their heads away from Rome and headed south across the great waters of the Mediterranean Sea towards the country of Mitsrayim (Egypt). They stopped and hovered over the city of Leontopolis. Leontopolis was also known as Heliopolis and was the ancient city of On. This was the same ancient city of the nativity of the daughter of the Priest of On that was given to Yowceph ben Yishra'Yah (Joseph son of Israel) by Par'oh (Pharaoh) around 1880 B.C. This union produced two sons, Mnashsheh and Ephrayim which became two tribes within the inheritance of the conquest of the land by the nation of Yisra'Yah (Israel). Today in 88 B.C. it was controlled by the tribe of Yhuwdah (Judah) under the leadership of Alexander Jannaeus. This city was a spiritual stronghold of Satan as it daily capitulated the will of the dark lord. Leontopolis (Heliopolis) was known as the chief cult center of the sun god Ra whom the Egyptians believed was the creator of all forms of life by calling them into existence as he spoke their secret names. The Hellene (Greek) dynasty renamed it Heliopolis after their sun god Apollo (Helios). But why were the minions of wickedness sent by their dark lord, Satan focused on the Hebrew-Egyptian Temple in this city today in 88 B.C.? Sadducee Rabbi Boethus was now twenty-one years old and had just sired his second son and named him Phabet. The black serpents were ready to inject their poison of deception, murder and lust for power into him with their stingers, just as they had done to his two-year old brother, Ananelus II, when out of nowhere came the whirring of the blazing sword of Yahuah Yahusha with its blinding light. The black serpents screamed in immense pain and beat a hasty retreat with their venomous tails tucked under them back to Rome and Yhuwdah (Judea). The dark lord, Satan cursed Yahuah Yahusha and rocked the underworld screaming, "He was mine, only mine! I will be the lord of light, you just wait and see!" Two massive angels were stationed over the newborn child, one on Phabet's right and one on Phabet's left. The pre-dawn Light of the World began to show brighter over the second child of the Sadducee Rabbi Boethus. Who was this child that Yahuah Yahusha gave angelic protection to? Why was the dark lord, Satan so upset over this defeat in the 'City of the Sun"? What did this birth have to do with the Roman Republic and the Hebrew territory of Yhuwdah (Judea)?

Nine years later in 79 B.C. the Vulture of Death began to head back towards the territory of Yhuwdah (Judea). King Alexander Jannaeus increased his already heavy drinking. He contacted malaria and was plagued with it over the next three years. King Alexander along with his Queen Alexandra Salome marched his army towards the city of Gaza, Palestine and struck a phony league of friendship with the Egyptian co-ruler Ptolomee XII Lathyrus. The massive Hebrew army withdrew under the orders of King Alexander Jannaeus and as they were leaving Ptolomee XII Lathyrus attacked a small Hebrew village with utter malice. The Egyptian troops strangled women and children. Then the deceased were cut into pieces, boiled in cauldrons and eaten as a sacrifice. This act of cannibalism terrified the people of Yhuwdah (Judea) and infuriated the Pharisees proclaiming their deaths and demonic sacrifice were a result of a scheme set up by King Alexander.

Three years later, in 76 B.C. King Alexander Jannaeus once again accompanied by Queen Alexandra Salome was warring against a northern city of Ragaba. Before the battle was completed he called Queen Alexandra Salome to his deathbed and instructed his wife to dismiss all of his Sadducee advisors and to reign as Queen with the aid of the Pharisees giving them more power. King Alexander said to his wife and Queen, "And so when you come to the great city of Yruwshalaim, send for the leading men among them, and show them my body; and with a great appearance of sincerity, give them leave to do with it as they please. Whether they will dishonor it by refusing it burial, because they have severely suffered by my actions, or whether in their anger they will offer it any other injury. Then promise them also that you will do nothing in the affairs of the kingdom without their consent. If you say this to them, then I shall have the honor of a more glorious funeral from them than you could have made for me; and when it is in their power to abuse my dead body they will do it no injury at all; and you will rule securely." Then King Alexander Jannaeus Maccabim, little "Yannai" (Johnny), died at the age of forty-nine years old and had reigned over the Hebrew people in Yhuwdah (Judea) for twenty-seven years. Then he died and she hid her husband's death from his soldiers and she led them to victory. She brought his body back to the great city of Yruwshalaim and did as he instructed by shifting the political power to the Pharisees. The Pharisees, who had the support of the general populace at that time, eulogized Alexander Jannaeus Maccabim and provided him an honorable burial as a national hero.

Thus in 76 B.C. Queen Alexandra Salome, who was now sixty-four years old, ascended to the throne as Queen of the Hebrew people, at the death of her husband. Since she was a woman, she could not serve as *Gadowl Kohen*, High Priest. Therefore, she appointed her oldest son, Hyrcanus II to serve as High Priest and her youngest son, Aristobulus II was appointed as Commander-in-Chief of the military. The reign of Alexandra was characterized as being extremely pro-Pharisee as her brother Pharisee Rabbi Simeon ben Shetah was still the leader of that party. The Pharisees severely persecuted the Saducees even getting permission from the Queen to use the Commander-in-Chief of the military to execute some of them. This infuriated Aristobulus II and he refused the orders of the Queen because he was sympathetic to the Sadducees like his father. Unlike her ruthless husband, she was loved by the Hebrew people and there was peace and prosperity during her reign. During the final years of her life she enjoyed spending time with her three grandchildren, beautiful little Alexandra the daughter of Hyrcanus II and her two rambunctious grandsons Alexander and Antigonus Matityahu, sons of Aristobulus II.

During her nine year rule Yhuwdah enjoyed prosperity granted by Yahuah Yahusha. The revolving sword returned to Yhuwdah (Judea) at the death of her husband King Alexander Jannaeus and did not allow the wicked minions to torture her with their infectious poison. The evil minions were chased back to Rome except for those who challenged the revolving sword and were gravely injured. They limped back to the black cauldron of Satan with their tails of poison tucked in defeat. Yahuah Yahusha permitted rain to fall only on Sabbath (Friday) nights so that the working class suffered no loss of pay through the rain falling during their work-time. The fertility of the soil was so great that the grains of wheat grew as large as kidney beans and the oats were as large as olives. The red lentils were as large as gold denarii and none of the goats, cattle or sheep suffered miscarriages. Then at the age of seventy-three years old in 67 B.C. Queen Alexandra Salome became gravely ill. The Pharisees fearing the military power of Aristobulus II and his loyalty to the Sadducees, conspired and convinced Hyrcanus II *HaGadowl Kohen*, the High Priest, to plead with his mother, the Queen and warn her about his brother's aggressive behavior. Therefore, Hyrcanus II along with her brother Pharisee Rabbi Simeon ben Shetah came before the Queen Alexandra Salome at her bedside and begged her to arrest and imprison her younger son Aristobulus II and hold them hostage in the Baris, the royal prison next to the Temple. She said, "Go ahead, I bid you to do what you think is proper to be done because you have many circumstances in your favor remaining even though Aristobulus II controls the fortresses. I leave to you a nation in sound condition, an army that other nations fear and a large quantity of money in several treasuries. Right now I have a small concern about public affairs, as the strength of my body is nearly gone." Not long after she had spoken these words, she died, when she had reined nine years, and had in all lived seventy-three. However, hours after her death, the wife and children of Aristobulus II were imprisoned in the Baris next to the Temple.

Because of the hatred of the two brothers, Hyrcanus II and Aristobulus II, sons of deceased King Alexander Jannaeus and Queen Alexandra Salome and the two warring factions of the religious parties of the Pharisees and Sadducees, the evil cauldron of Satan began brewing and billowing dark loathsome wickedness once again in 67 B.C. This lack of love for one another in Yhuwdah (Judea) drove out the pre-dawn light of the Son-Rise on High and Yahuah Yahusha withdrew the revolving sword with its deafening whirring sound and its blinding pure light. The legions of evil minions of Satan screamed and howled as they left the smoke of the bellowing cauldron. Some joined forces over the Roman Republic of Rome, others scurried to Antioch, Syria, more descended upon Leontopolis, Mitsrayim (Egypt), and some of the strongest minions attacked the territory of Yhuwdah (Judea) and the great city of Yruwshalaim (Jerusalem) with their stings of poison filled with greed, murder and deception. How could mankind survive such a widespread attack? What was the common thread that would bring all these territories together in history? Was the dark lord Satan finally going to claim victory over mankind? Where was the Vulture of Death going to sink its blood-thirsty talons next?

II

The Roman Republic found itself in turmoil from 79 B.C. to 67 B.C. because Dictator Lucius Cornelius Sulla resigned his dictatorship and then died in 78 B.C. at his villa outside the city of Puteoli, Italy. This allowed Julius Caesar to come back to Rome and Pompey to leave Rome and begin his military campaign in the territory of Spain. Marcus Antonius, the cousin of Julius Caesar joined Pompey and became one of his commanders becoming a spy for Julius Caesar. The Roman Senate was so impressed once again with General Pompey that they gave him a Senate seat which he fulfilled *in absentia*, in the absence of his presence so he could continue his military campaigns. The Senate also gave him *imperium*, entire authority and control of the navy in the waters of the Mediterranean Sea to battle pirates.

After returning from Spain with Marcus Antonius and before leaving to battle the pirates on the waters of the Mediterranean Sea, Pompey formed a political alliance called a *Trimvirate*, 'rule of three men', with his enemy General Marcus Licinius Crassus and with his ally Julius Caesar. This *Trimvirate*, allowed the three unlimited power, wealth and political status and essentially control of the development of the Roman Republic. To solidify this agreement Pompey divorced his third wife Mucia Tertia for adultery. Before he had left for Spain after the death of Dictator Sulla he had divorced his second wife, Aemelia Scaura the step-daughter of Dictator Sulla and married Mucia Tertia. Now to validate the agreement with Julius Caesar, Pompey married Caesar's daughter Julia and then left to do battle with the pirates. After successfully defeating the pirates on the waters of the Mediterranean Sea his thirst for power grew larger and he decided to take his army with Marcus Antonius at his side and take over the territory of Syria from his old enemy General Crassus and add Syria as a province to the Roman Republic. However, first he would have to squelch the uprising and continual battles of northeast Turkey before he could successfully march into Syria. His ultimate plan was to assume the vacant seat of Dictator, left by the death of Dictator Sulla and with his planned victories in the East the Senate would not have any choice but to give him the throne of the Roman Republic. The poison of greed and quest for power was taking its effect.

In the meantime, during this same period of time, Julius Caesar had his own intentions to shape the future of the Roman Republic. Hearing of Dictator Sulla's death in 78 B.C. Julius Caesar felt safe enough to return to Rome. However, he lacked financial means since the inheritance of his extremely wealthy father and aristocrat mother was confiscated, he acquired a modest house in the lower-class neighborhood of Rome. Then he decided to turn to legal advocacy and became known for his exceptional oratory skills accompanied by impassioned gestures and a high-pitched voice. His tall stature with a fair complexion, shapely muscular limbs and a full face with keen black eyes mesmerized his audiences. In 77 B.C. he began his successful prosecution of former governors notorious for extortion and corruption. His first legal case was to persecute the governor of the territory of Macedonia (Northern Greece), General Cornelius Dolabella Minor, which Caesar won decisively. Due to his successful oratory legal victories, the Roman Senate elected him as *tribunes militum*, Tribune of the Military, which put him in charge of a legion of three-thousand men. This was the first crucial step of his intended political career.

Then in 69 B.C. Julius Caesar was elected by the Senate to be a *quaestor*, a person who handled the financial affairs of the Roman Republic. That year he delivered the funeral oration for his aunt Julia, his father's sister and his wife, Cornelia also died. After successfully serving his term as *quaestor*, The Senate in 68 B.C. elected him to a one year term as *praetorium ius*, magistrate of the law, in the territory of Spain. However, Julius Caesar was still in considerable debt and needed to satisfy his creditors before he could leave to be governor. Therefore he turned to General Marcus Licinius Crassus, one of Rome's richest men. In return for political support in General Crassus's opposition to the interests of Pompey, he paid off some of Caesar's debts and acted as a guarantor for the rest. Julius Caesar was still deeply in debt and knew that there was a large amount of money to be made as a governor, whether by extortion or by military adventurism. As *praetorium ius* and *tribunes militum*, he now had four entire legions of twelve-thousand soldiers under his command to do his bidding. When his term was over, he returned to Rome in 67 B.C. and married Pompeia Sulla, a granddaughter of dead Dictator Sulla and relative of Pompey, whom he later divorced that year. Julius Caesar married again, this time to Callpurnia the daughter of another powerful senator. Then in 63 B.C., he ran for the post of *Pontifex Maximus*, chief priest of the Roman state religion. Julius Caesar won comfortably miraculously by the help of the dark lord over two opponents with greater experience and political standing. Also, this year Julius Caesar celebrated the birth of his grand-nephew and adopted son, Gaius Octavaius Augustus. So while General Pompey was having success in his military campaigns to gain the throne of the Roman Republic, Julius Caesar was conquering the political battlefield as well as amassing military might of his own. The wicked bestial poison of greed and power ran thick in their veins deceiving each other and ultimately themselves. The pre-dawn light was getting dimmer as each morning sky turned darker with black storm clouds of wickedness.

In 69 B.C. events in Mitsrayim (Egypt) added to the drama that was playing out on the stage of the future existence of mankind. Ptolomee XII Lathyrus produced a daughter and crowned her Queen. He named her Cleopatra. This was the same Ptolomee that had murdered the Hebrews in a small village of Yhuwdah (Judea) and then ate their flesh as a sacrifice to the sun god Ra ten years ago. Also, in the cult city of Leontopolis (Heliopolis) dedicated to the sun god Ra, Phabet ben Boethus sired his oldest son, Pharisee Rabbi Yhowshuwa III ben Phabet, meaning 'Yahuah Saved'. Phabet would go on to sire two more sons, Eliam and Sadducee Rabbi Ishmael I. Even though Pharisee Rabbi Yhowshuwa III ben Phabet was born in Mitsrayim (Egypt) he became very important to the pre-dawn light of Yahuah Yahusha. Sadducee Rabbi Boethus ben Ananelus would go on to sire a total of seven sons: first, Ananelus II ben Boethus; second, Phabet ben Boethus; third, Simon IV ben Boethus; forth, Joazar ben Boethus: fifth, Eleazar ben Boethus; sixth, Sethus ben Boethus; and seventh, Kantharas ben Boethus. These Hebrew sons born in exile in Mitsrayim (Egypt) would sire children that would change the landscape of religious worship for centuries of generations to come. Why were they so important as history changers? Who were their children? Were they part of the dark storm clouds of wickedness or will they join Yahuah Yahusha in the fight to part the storm clouds to allow room for the pre-dawn light?

Following the death of Alexandra, Queen of the territory Yhuwdah (Judea), in 67 B.C., her son Yhowchanan Hyrcanus II *Gadowl Kohen,* High Priest and a strong supporter of the Pharisees ascended to the throne. This created a civil war in the land of

Yhuwdah (Judea) because the Queen's youngest son, Aristobulus II who was Commander-in-Chief of the military and a strong supporter of the Sadducees, knew his older brother was not mentally capable of ruling a country and was just a puppet of the Pharisees. Within three months, Aristobulus II led an army of twenty-five thousand *gammedim,* warriors, backed by the Sadducees against the great city of Yruwshalaim in an effort to take the throne by force from his brother. This caught Hyrcanus II and the Pharisees by surprise and they yielded the throne without a fight. Then Aristobulus II became both King and *Gadowl Koen*, High Priest, with the power of the Sanhedrin back in control of the Sadducees.

That same year Hyrcanus II gave his only daughter in marriage to *Nasi*, Prince Matityahu ben Levi who was nicknamed "Mattat". Prince Matityahu ben Levi came from the most powerful family in the tribe of Yhuwdah (Judah) who supported the Pharisees. He was thirty-ninth in the line of Davidic Kings and the seventy-third generation from Adam, the first man created by Yahuah Yahusha. The daughter's Hebrew name was Elizabeth of Yruwshalaim but her Greek and Regal name was Princess Alexandra II. This union produced a son in 66 B.C. and his Hebrew name was Eliy ben Matityahu but his Regal Greek name was Prince Alexander Helios III. His father nicknamed him "Heli". Then in 65 B.C. his sister was born, Princess Alexandra III. Towards the end of that year Hyrcanus II feared for his life at the constant insistence of the Pharisees, who convinced him to flee south to the Nabataeans (Arabs). His son-in-law Prince Matityahu ben Levi fearing a civil war between the Pharisees and the Sadducees fled to Leontopolis (Heliopolis) Mitsrayim (Egypt) with his infant son and daughter. His wife Alexandra II refused to go with him and fled south to the Nabataens (Arabs) with her father.

While Hyrcanus II was with the Nabataens (Arabs) he met a

man by the name of Herod Antipater I the Idumean. He was the son of Governor Antipas, the governor of Idumea (Edom). Antipater I with the funding of the Pharisees became the advisor for Hyrcanus II. Antipater I saw in this situation an opportunity to fulfill his own dream of avenging his grandfather's death, which was at the hands of the Maccabim family and gain the throne of Yhuwdah (Judea) himself. Therefore, he convinced the weaker brother, Hyrcanus II to return to the great city of Yruwshalaim (Jerushalaim) and try to gain the favor of his brother. Thus, Hyrcanus II returned to his brother Aristobulus II to make peace. The two brothers decided to make a vow of 'eternal friendship' with one another and this vow was sealed with the marriage of Alexander, the oldest son of Aristobulus II and the previously married daughter Princess Alexandra II, his cousin and the only daughter of Hyrcanus II. This 'eternal friendship' was short-lived as hostilities soon broke out between the two brothers fueled by the Sadducees and the Pharisees. Once again, Hyrcanus II was eventually forced to flee for his life back to the Nabataens (Arabs) with his advisor Herod Antipater I.

Then in 63 B.C. Herod Antipater I persuaded Hyrcanus II that he needed to return to Yhuwdah and reclaim the throne which should be friendly to the Pharisees, like his mother the Queen had established, not the Sadducees friends of his brother. Herod Antipater I also convinced the Arabs to send a large army with Hyrcanus II in order to help him achieve this goal with the funding coming from the Pharisees in Yruwshalaim. Then the Arab army of fifty-thousand soldiers, funded by Yruwshalaim Hebrew Pharisees laid siege to the great city of Yruwshalaim for several months. Fear of a major civil war concerned the inhabitants of the great city of Yruwshalaim including Melek' Beyth Aer (Henry Ayers), the fan maker in the Upper City because he was now a proud father of a newborn son, Yhowchanan ben Melek'Beyth Aer (John Henry Ayers).

A year earlier, General Pompey marched into Syria and killed its king, Antiochus XIII Asiaticus and made it a Roman Province. Now word reached his ears and the Roman Republic of this civil war of the Hebrews in Yhuwdah and was intrigued with the situation. Therefore, he was ordered by the Senate to move his army south and intervene in the civil war and re-establish peace in this territory. When General Pompey arrived at the great city of Yruwshalaim both sides presented their case to him, each hoping the general and his vast Roman army would come to their aid. In the end, Pompey ruled in favor of Hyrcanus II and the Pharisees and declared him the rightful heir to the throne, deeming the elder the weaker brother a more reliable ally of the Roman Republic. Aristobulus II refused to submit to this decision so Pompey and his Roman army and Hyrcanus II with his Arab army attacked the city of Yruwshalaim. The battle lasted another three months and after twelve-thousand Hebrews loyal to the Sadducees died defending the city, the city finally fell. Pompey reinstated Hyrcanus II as *Gadowl Kohen*, High Priest with no political power and Herod Antipater I was made Minister of the territory of Yhuwdah. Then the Roman Senate declared the Hasmonean Dynasty to be terminated and Yhuwdah as a province of the increasingly powerful Roman Republic. Marcus Antonius who was commander of the cavalry captured Aristobulus II and his oldest son Alexander and took them back to Antioch, Syria as prisoners. Before Alexander was taken prisoner, he sired a daughter, Mariamne I with Alexandra II. General Pompey returned to Rome and arrived back home in 62 B.C.

The news of Pompey's victories in the east reached Rome before he did and the people of the Roman Republic began a cult and called him "savior". While Pompey was absent from Rome on his military campaigns, his old supporter Cicero had risen to consulship and his old enemy and colleague General Crassus supported Julius Caesar. Even though only half of the Roman Senate supported him over Julius Caesar, on the streets he was as popular as ever. On his 45th birthday in 61 B.C. he rode the triumphal chariot proclaiming him as magnificent god-king as he was accompanied by a gigantic portrait head of himself studded with pearls. The consulship of Julius Caesar in 59 B.C. persuaded the Senate to give the governorship of Hispania (Spain) to Pompey but he remained in Rome to oversee the grain supply as *curator amnonae*, grain buyer. Despite his preoccupation with his wife, Julia the only child of Julius Caesar, Pompey handled the grain issue very well. He also was busy with his planning a new grand theatre to be built in his name. Meanwhile Julius Caesar seemed set on outstripping General Pompey and General Crassus in generalship and popularity. By 56 B.C. the bonds between the three most powerful and wealthiest men in Rome were fraying. Caesar called them both to a secret meeting in the northern Italian town of Lucca to rethink their joint strategy. They agreed that Pompey would keep the governorship of Hispania (Spain) *in absentia*, in absence, and remain in Rome. General Crassus would have the influential and lucrative governorship of Syria and use the base to conquer Parthia (Persia-modern Iran). All the while, Caesar would begin a conquest of Gaul (France) and Britain with thirteen legions of soldiers.

The following year, in 55 BC, Pompey and Crassus were elected as consuls, against a background of bribery, civil unrest and electioneering violence. General Crassus left for Syria with his son and Julius Caesar headed to Britain. Pompey's new grand theatre was inaugurated in the same year. It was Rome's first permanent theatre, a gigantic, architecturally daring, self-contained complex on the Campus Martius complete with shops, multi-service buildings, gardens and a temple to Venus. In its portico, the statuary, paintings and personal wealth of foreign kings could be admired at leisure. Pompey's triumph lived on and his theatre made an ideal meeting place for his supporters. While Caesar was in Britain that year, his daughter Julia, Pompey's wife died in childbirth along with her baby. Julia's death broke the family bonds between Caesar and Pompey and Caesar sought a second matrimonial alliance with Pompey by offering his grand-niece, the sister of Octavian Augustus. General Pompey snubbed Julius Caesar and with contempt refused the offer of Julius Caesar. The next year General Crassus and his son Publius were killed in battle and most of his army was annihilated by the soldiers of Parthia (Persia-modern Iran). Then Pompey married Cornelia Metella, the very young widow of Publius and daughter of Caecilius Metellus Scipio, one of Caesar's greatest enemies in the Roman Senate. Julius Caesar completed his conquests of Gaul (France) and Britain with unmatched military power and threatened the military accomplishments of General Pompey. With the death of General Crassus, political realignments took place in Rome and finally led to a standoff between General Caesar and General Pompey. Therefore, Pompey took up his cause in the Senate which ordered Caesar to return to Rome to stand trial for insubordination and treason if he did not disband his army.

As the Roman Republic was in a power struggle between two greedy Generals, the new Roman province of Yhuwdah (Judea) had its own challenges. Aristobulus II and his son Alexander escaped from prison in Antioch, Syria. While they were on their way back to Yhuwdah, Marcus Antonius caught up with them in 49 B.C. and captured them before they could get to the great city of Yruwshalaim. He poisoned Aristobulus II and made Alexander watch his father die a very painful death. However, Alexander was taken back to Antioch, Syria and beheaded in a public execution. Hyrcanus II continued as *Gadowl Kohen*, High Priest while Herod Antipater continued to rule as Minister of the territory. Hyrcanus II wanted to solidify his friendship with Herod Antipater so he gave his granddaughter, Mariamne I to the second son of Herod Antipater, Herod the Great as his second wife. Now with Aristobulus II and his son dead, the Sadducees were left powerless and were greatly persecuted by the Pharisees. However, the Herod family was at odds with the Pharisees and lent their favor to the outnumbered Sadducees. Without the power of the throne the Herod's were powerless to help the Sadducees. When Alexandra II learned of her husband Alexander's death she quickly took their three year old son, Aristobulus III and married the youngest son of Aristobulus II, Antigonus Matityahu Maccabim and this union produced a daughter, Antigone. The Sadducee family of Onais V far away across the desert in Leontopolis (Heliopolis) Mitsrayim (Egypt) continued to grow. Yhowshuwa III (Joshua) ben Phabet sired two of his three daughters. The oldest was Yehanne (Jane) and the second daughter was Elizabeth. Also, Ishmael I ben Phabet sired a son who was named Gamaliel and he became one of the most famous Rabbis in Hebrew history.

Far beyond the evil churning storm clouds of wickedness that hovered above the earth, there came into appearance a small dot of bright shining pure light like a speck in the vast ocean of dark outer space. The evil minions of Satan began to grow nervous but did not understand why because things on the earth were a mess just as their dark lord had planned. What was that small speck of pure light and why was it so powerful? One of the demonic captains called forth two of the strongest demons that were stationed over the territory of Yhuwdah (Judea) and said, "You two wicked beasts are no longer assigned to torment mankind but you have an important mission to ensure the victory for the dark lord, Satan. Watch that speck of pure light night and day. If it moves or appears to get closer, you must report to Satan immediately. If you fail this mission you will be placed in an arid place of no moisture where you will wander aimlessly in pain and misery as punishment for eternity. Now get to your posts!"

Several evil beasts tried to attack the family of Rabbi Yhowshuwa III (Joshua) however, just as before whenever they tried to inject their poison of deceit, murder and an unquenchable thirst for power and greed, they were met immediately by the whirling and rotating swift sword of Yahweh Yahshua. No matter how hard they fought the swift whirling sword would inflict deep wounds causing immense pain and they would have to beat a hasty retreat. Why was this Rabbi in Leontopolis (Heliopolis), Mitsrayim (Egypt) so special to receive the protection of Yahuah Yahusha? Even when lesser demons of disease or deformities tried to attack the two small daughters of Rabbi Yhowshuwa III (Joshua), they were turned away by that rotating swift sword of Yahuah Yahusha. Why was Yehanne (Jane) and Elizabeth so important? They did not appear to be any different than any of the other Hebrew daughters in Mitsrayim (Egypt) or even Yhuwdah (Judea) for that matter. Were special husbands and history-making children awaiting them in their future destiny when they got older? No matter what the questions, we know that in the pre-dawn light these two girls have divine security.

The dark lord, Satan, returned from roaming on the earth to the boiling evil cauldron of darkness. He was very agitated and his hatred for Yahuah Yahusha glowed red like burning embers of coal. He let out such a loud eerie scream that all the demonic beings on the earth cowered like whipped puppies and his lieutenant commanders scampered back to him through the dark spiritual world at top speed. When the last lieutenant commander arrived, who had been assigned over Rome, the nostrils of the great serpent of old, Satan, breathed smoke and fire and his eyes glowed like bottomless chasms of boiling lava. The dark lord lashed out with his sharp talons at the helpless lieutenant commander causing deep lacerations across its chest and throat. Black putrid slime oozed from the filthy wounds filling the air with the odor of rotting flesh and death. The fangs of the other demonic lieutenant commanders dripped with saliva as they waited for the command of the dark lord to pounce upon the mortally wounded beast. However, the command never came from the dark lord and the wounded beast slumped to the ground in a whimpering heap pleading for mercy but none was shown. Then the dark lord, Satan raged in a torrent of fury, "Don't you ever be last when I summon you! How dare any of you feel it is ok to be last when my victory is at hand! Yahuah Yahusha is up to something but I do not know what it is. I will defeat Him and I will reign on His throne but not if you incompetent excuses for fallen angels continue to think it is ok to be last! My chosen one in Rome, General Julius Caesar, my high priest, is about to be defeated by General Pompey and you all stand by and do nothing. I want all forces to make sure that Julius Caesar controls Rome. He is my vessel to control time and eventually the foundation for religious worship for all mankind on the face of the earth. Yet, you bumbling good-for-nothings are going to ruin everything! Now go and poison the Senate, causing as much discord as possible, spread hatred and deceit, and above all do not fail me! I am the lord of the earth and I am due the worship of all mankind. I will rule heaven and earth forever!"

12

General Julius Caesar who was *Pontifex Maximus*, chief priest of the Roman religion, complied with the request of General Pompey and the Roman Senate and returned to Rome. However, he did not disband his army as ordered and give up his authority as *imperium*, the right to command. It was Roman law that only elected officials could lead an army within Italy and only in their assigned territories. General Caesar was not elected to be commander within the city limits of Rome. Therefore, by not disbanding his army he and his army was in direct violation of the laws of Rome and were committing a capital offence, punishable by death. If he and his army entered Rome then they would be considered outlaws and were automatically condemned to death without a trial or legal defense. The Rubicon River stood between them and Rome.

On January 10th, 49 B.C. General and *Pontifex Maximus*, Julius Caesar led his Legion XIII from Gaul to Italy. He crossed the river Rubicon, which is a shallow red river thus its name *rubeus*, meaning red. General Pompey and most of the Roman Senate fled Rome for their safety and did not even challenge the powerful General and *Pontifex Maximus*, chief priest, Julius Caesar. Now that he was in control of Rome, Caesar was appointed as Dictator and Marcus Antonius (Mark Anthony) as his *Magister Equitum,* Master of the Horse (second in command). Julius Caesar next presided over his own election to a second consulship and then after eleven days resigned this dictatorship so he could pursue General Pompey who was fleeing to Mitsrayim (Egypt).

General Pompey and his family reached the shores of the Nile River delta in Mitsrayim (Egypt) where he was met by a welcoming party sent by Ptolomee XII Lathyrus. Pompey's wife and children were taken to the shore but Ptolomee sent word to him that General Caesar was on his way to Mitsrayim (Egypt) and Pompey needed to be taken to a place of safety. Six of Ptolomee's body guards got into the boat and began rowing away from the shore as Pompey's wife and children waved goodbye. When they got a good distance from the shoreline, the six Mitsrayim (Egyptian) body guards dropped their oars, gripped their daggers and began repeatedly stabbing the helpless and surprised General Pompey. As life was literally pouring out of him, he was rowed back to shore and his wife ran horrified to the boat. As she embraced her dying husband he said, *"et Dues Roma datum"*, a god of Rome has died. Then General Pompey gasped his last breath in the early spring of 49 B.C. and died in her now bloody arms. His lifeless body was drug from the little boat and laid on the shore like a prized game animal. Then at the command of Ptolomee XII Lathyrus, his son Ptolomee XIII drew his sword from his scabbard and beheaded General Pompey to serve as a trophy.

General Julius Caesar and his Legion XIII finally arrived in Mitsrayim (Egypt) seeking out General Pompey. A welcoming party met him and took him to the palace of Ptolomee XII Lathyrus. Those going to the palace were Julius Caesar, Marcus Antonius along with their body guards as the feared Legion XIII remained in the warships offshore. As they entered the Great Hall, at the end of the center isle was Pharaoh Ptolomee XII Lathyrus sitting on a large golden inlaid throne with his son on his right. His beautiful daughter regent-Queen Cleopatra was on his left adorned with her blue-painted eyes, silk wrap-around dress and shimming gold accenting her beautiful features. General Caesar and Marcus Antonius bowed their heads and with their right arms hit their left shoulders with right clinched fists. Then General Caesar spoke yet his eyes were glued to Cleopatra, "King Ptolomee XII Lathyrus, as you are the authority of the land of Mitsrayim (Egypt) which is a territory of the Roman Republic and I am the leader of the Roman Republic, I request your assistance of rooting out a criminal of Rome abiding within your borders seeking your protection. I will not withdraw my army from your shores until General Pompey is dead in my presence." Ptolomee XII Lathyrus smiled at Julius Caesar who was mezmorized by the entrancing beauty of Cleopatra and replied, "Commander Caesar, I know full well of your world-renown military victories and your position of leadership in Rome. Your wish is my command as I am here as your servant and great ally. I have a gift for you to show my loyalty to your future ambitions."

Then Pharaoh Ptolomee XII Lathyrus stomped his long golden sepulcher on the royal platform and two servants quickly left the room. Within minutes the two servants returned to the Great Hall carrying a red pillow with a reed-woven basket covered with a red silk cloth. Then they placed it at the feet of General Julius Caesar and removed the red silk cloth covering the wicker basket. General Caesar peered into the basket, gasped and then fell to his knees weeping. Marcus Antonius quickly looked inside the wicker basket to find the lifeless head of the defeated great General Pompey. Cleopatra descended from the platform, put a tender hand on the head of General Julius Caesar and commanded, "Get this thing out of here now!" The two servants obeyed.

Later that evening, Julius Caesar met with Marcus Antonius after inquiring from palace servants how General Pompey had been captured so easily. While they were discussing possible retributions against the throne of Mitsrayim (Egypt) for murdering a Roman Official without a *decretum,* decree from Rome, a rapid and repeated knock came from the door of their chambers. When Marcus Antonius answered and opened the door, wailing and hustling about could be heard throughout the long halls. A royal servant quickly muttered as the Roman body guards watched cautiously, "Pharaoh Ptolomee XII Lathyrus has died in his bed chambers!" Then the royal servant hurried away as Marcus Antonius shut the door in disbelief. Julius Caesar and Marcus Antonius devised a plan that would be put into action after the official burial in the pyramids of the great kings of Egypt. General Julius Caesar put his personal guards at the door on full alert and sent word to the warships of the Legion XIII to stand ready for war.

After the funeral, Julius Caesar warmed up to and comforted Cleopatra as Marcus Antonius bent the ears of her brothers Ptolomee XIII and Ptolomee XIV telling them that Cleopatra was scheming to murder them and use Julius Caesar and his powerful Legion XIII to secure the throne of Mitsrayim (Egypt) for herself. For many days the two brothers watched the eye contact and body gestures between their sister Cleopatra and the google-eyed Julius Caesar. Finally, at the end of the week Ptolomee XIII and Ptolomee XIV gathered all their armies by the Nile River ready to march on the royal city of Alexandria at the end of the month. General Julius Caesar acting in a ploy of being the protective hero towards Cleopatra, offered his protection towards her by mobilizing his Legion XIII around the city of Alexandria under the command of Marcus Antonius. The Egyptian armies of the two younger brothers were crushed by the mighty Legion XIII of Julius Caesar in 47 B.C. and they were killed in battle. After a brief mourning period Caesar and Cleopatra celebrated their victory with a triumphant procession on the Nile River in the spring of 47 B.C. The royal barge was accompanied by 400 additional ships, and Caesar was introduced to the luxurious lifestyle of the Egyptian pharaohs. Caesar and Cleopatra never married, as Roman law recognized marriages only between two Roman citizens. Caesar continued his relationship with Cleopatra throughout his last marriage, which lasted fourteen years and in Roman eyes, this did not constitute adultery. Queen Cleopatra visited Rome on more than one occasion, residing in Caesar's villa just outside Rome across the Tiber River. Before General Julius Caesar and Marcus Antonius returned to Rome late that year, Julius Caesar declared Queen Cleopatra as the sole authority in Alexandria, Mitsrayim (Egypt) and she gave birth to a son and named him Ptolomee XV Caesarion, after his father Julius Caesar.

After Julius Caesar returned to Rome Italy in early 46 B.C., he assumed control of the government and began extensive reforms of Roman society and government. First, he changed the government from a Roman Republic to a Roman Empire and was proclaimed *dictatum perpetualis*, dictator in perpetuity (Eternal Dictator). He also changed the calendar of time which was regulated by the movement of the moon. Caesar replaced the calendar with the Mitsrayim (Egyptian) calendar which was regulated by the sun in the city of Leontopolis (Heliopolis) Egypt, the City of the Sun. He also named the first six months after Roman gods since he was still *Pontifex Maximus*, chief priest of the Roman religion and the seventh month, the month of his birth, after himself as Julius or July. The calendar was commanded to be known as the Julian calendar and opened on January 1, 45 B.C. He was given a special chair in the Senate and was offered a form of semi-official cult so he named Marcus Antonius as *Pontifex Maximus*, high priest. In September 45 B.C. Emperor

Caesar filed his will naming his grandnephew fifteen-year old Gaius Octavius (Octavian) Augustus as the heir to everything, including his name of Caesar. The Emperor also wrote that if Octavian died before Caesar did, then young Marcus Junius Brutus would be the next heir in succession, not the cousin of Caesar, Marcus Antonius. Over the next eight months Emperor Julius Caesar suffered from acute migraine headaches from his bouts of malaria causing him to convulse in seizures and on occasions to lose consciousness.

Then on the Ides of March, March 15th of 44 BC, Caesar was due to appear at a special session of the Senate. Marcus Antonius having vaguely learned of the plot the night before from a terrified informant and fearing the worst, went to head Caesar off. The plotters, however, had anticipated this fearing that Antonius would come to Caesar's aid, had arranged for Senator Trebonius to intercept him just as he approached the portico of the grand Theater of Pompey where the session was to be held, and detain him outside. However, when Caesar arrived at the Senate, Senator Tillius Cimber presented him with a petition to recall his exiled brother while the other conspirators crowded around to offer support of the petition. Caesar waved him away, but Senator Cimber grabbed his shoulders and pulled down the tunic of Caesar. Then Caesar cried, *"Ista Quidem vis est!"*, Why this violence! At the same time Senator Casca produced his dagger and made a glancing thrust at the neck of Emperor Caesar. However, Caesar turned around quickly and caught Casca by the arm and said, "Casca you villain, what are you doing?" Then frightened Casca shouted to Marcus Junius Brutus, the son of Caesar's favorite mistress, *"adelphe, boether!"* Help brother! When Marcus Antonius heard the commotion inside the chamber he fled the scene.

Within moments, the entire group, including Brutus, was striking out at the Emperor. Caesar attempted to get away but blinded by blood, he tripped and fell. The men continued stabbing him as he lay defenseless on the lower steps of the portico. He was stabbed twenty-three times with the last one being a second fatal wound to his chest. Caesar's last words were, *"Kai su, teknon? Et tu, Brute?"* You too child? You too, Brutus? After the assassination, Marcus Junius Brutus stepped forward as if to say something to his fellow horrified senators but they fled the building. Brutus and his companions then marched to the Capitol while crying out to their beloved city, "People of Rome, we are once again free!" They were met with silence, as the citizens of Rome had locked themselves inside their houses as soon as the rumor of what had taken place had begun to spread. The dead body of Emperor Julius Caesar laid where it had fallen on the Senate floor for nearly three hours before the officials arrived to remove it. His body was cremated and later the Temple of Caesar was constructed on the east side of the main square of the Roman Forum on the exact site where his cremation took place. The crowd at the funeral boiled over, throwing dry branches, furniture and even clothing onto the funeral pyre of Caesar causing the flames to spin out of control, seriously damaging the Forum. The mob then attacked the houses of Brutus and Casca where they were repelled only with considerable difficulty. The day after the cremation, Marcus Antonius the cousin of the slain Emperor attended the reading of his will. However, to his surprise and chagrin, Caesar had named his grandnephew Gaius Octavian Augustus his sole heir, bequeathing him the immensely potent Caesar name and making him one of the wealthiest citizens in the Republic.

After a year of verbal battles in the Forum Gallorum between Octavian and Marcus Antonius, in 43 B.C. Marcus Antonius left with a legion of soldiers to hunt down Marcus Junius Brutus, who had fled to Gaul (France). By mid-summer Marcus Antonius caught up with Marcus Junius Brutus, the assassination planner of Emperor Julius Caesar, and killed him in battle. General Marcus Antonius returned to Rome in the early fall and began with the help of Emperor Octavian to lobby the Roman Senate to deify Julius Caesar, to make him a god causing the dark lord, Satan, to smile. Then on January 1st 42 B.C. the Roman Senate overwhelmingly voted to deify Julius Caesar beginning the Imperial Cult of Rome. With this formality of deification of Caesar making him as *Divus Julius*, god Julius then Caesar Octavian automatically became *Divi Filius*, Son of god as his adoptive heir. Marcus Antonius was sent to Antioch, Syria to run that province. While there he formed an alliance with Julius Caesar's lover, Queen Cleopatra, intending to use the fabulously wealthy Mitsrayim (Egypt) as a base to dominate Rome. Then in 37 B.C. Marcus Antonius divorced his wife, the sister of Caesar Octavian Augustus, and married Queen Cleopatra. This created a rift between Octavian Augustus as Caesar in Rome with Marcus Antonius ruling in Antioch, Syria and Queen Cleopatra ruling in Alexandria, Mitsrayim (Egypt). Queen Cleopatra had three children by Marcus Antonius, two sons and one daughter named Selene.

In the far away territory of Yhuwdah (Judea) during the same time frame of 49 B.C.-37 B.C., while Julius Caesar was in Mitsrayim (Egypt) he gave Hyrcanus II Maccabim the title of *ethnarch*, ruler of a nation. This action voided the position given to Herod Antipater as Minister of the land by General Pompey. Julius Caesar was an ally to the Hasmonean (Maccabim) family while the Herodian family supported General Pompey and the late General Cassius. This however had little practical effect since Hyrcanus II yielded to Herod Antipater in everything anyway. Therefore, that same year Herod Antipater served as Procurator and appointed twenty-five year old Herod the Great, his second son as governor of Galilee and his older brother Phasael as governor of the great city of Yruwshalaim. Herod the Great enjoyed the backing of Rome but his brutality was condemned by the Sanhedrin. Herod the Great considered himself royalty since his mother was Princess Cypros from Petra, Nabatea (Jordan). Everything was going the Herodians's way to take over the throne of Yhuwdah (Judea) from the Hasmoneans (Maccabim) six years later.

Procurator Herod Antipater was poisoned in 43 B.C. by a tax-collector because he helped fund the assassination of Emperor Julius Caesar. This caused great chaos in Yhuwdah so Herod the Great, backed by the Roman Army, executed the murderer of his father and towards the end of 42 B.C. he convinced General Marcus Antonius and Caesar Octavian Augustus that Herod Antipater had been forced to help the murderers of Julius Caesar. Therefore, when Marcus Antonius was stationed in Antioch, Syria he named Herod as the official *tetrarch*, Roman governor of Galilee. When Herod the Great returned home he banished his first wife Doris and her three-year-old son Antipater II so he could spend more time with his teenage wife Mariamne I Maccabim without the 'catty' remarks by his older and not as beautiful wife.

Two years later in 40 B.C. Antigonus II Matityahu Maccabim the nephew of Hyrcanus II took the throne from his uncle with the help of the Parthians (Persians–modern Iran). This made Herod the Great flee to Rome to plead with the Romans to restore him to power. There he was elected as 'King of the Jews" by the Roman Senate. Antigonus II Matityahu gained the adherence of the aristocratic class in the great city of Yruwshalaim (Jerusalem) and led a three year fierce struggle of the Hebrew people for independence from the Roman Empire. To prevent his inept uncle from acting as *Gadowl Kohen*, High Priest, Antigonus II Matityahu seized his uncle Hyrcanus II and bit his ears off, thus preventing Hyrcanus II from becoming *Gadowl Kohen*, High Priest ever again. Therefore, Hyrcanus II was banished to Babylon after suffering the mutilation of his ears.

Herod went back to Yhuwdah (Judea) in 39 B.C. to win his kingdom from Antigonus II Matityahu. In the spring of 38 B.C. Herod the Great wrestled control of the province of Galilee and eventually all of Palestine as far as the land surrounding the great city of Yruwshalaim (Jerusalem). Due to the approaching of winter, Herod the Great postponed his planned siege of the great city of Yruwshalaim, where Antigonus II Matityahu and the remnants of his army took refuge. Then during the spring of 37 B.C. Herod the Great attacked the great city and he and the Roman army was held off for five months. Eventually the Roman army broke the walls of the great city and Antigonus II Matityahu and his *gammedim*, warriors, fought until the Romans reached the inner courtyard of the Temple. King and *Gadowl Kohen*, High Priest, Antigonus II Matityahu Maccabim was captured, thus ending the Hasmonean Dynasty rule of Yhuwdah (Judea). He was taken to Antioch, Syria and turned over to General Marcus Antonius. The general stripped him naked and had him bound to a stake in the public square and had him scourged. A punishment that literally ripped the flesh of the victim off his body and the remaining flesh was shredded quivering ribbons and exposed sinew. No king had ever suffered such a horrific and humiliating punishment at the hands of the Roman Empire. Then Marcus Antonius had him beheaded and his headless body drug throughout Yhuwdah for one month and his head placed on a pole near the gates of the great city of Yruwshalaim as a reminder that the Roman Empire was now in charge of the Hebrew people.

With Herod the Great now sitting on the throne in Yruwshalaim, he needed a high priest. He did not trust his enemies the Pharisees on the Sanhedrin to elect one that supported his throne, since he was not of the Davidic Lineage. To make matters worse he was not even Hebrew but was half-Edomite and half-Arab. However, since he was married to a Hebrew he claimed that he had a right to the throne through his teenage Hebrew wife. The Pharisees and the Sanhedrin vehemently rejected this theory and protested. Therefore, Herod the Great sent word to the Hebrew Temple in Leontopolis (Heliopolis) Mitsrayim (Egypt) to Sadducee Rabbi Ananelus to return to the great city of Yruwshalaim with his family and assume the duties as the *Gadowl Kohen*, High Priest.

Sadducee Rabbi Ananelus (Hananeel the Egyptian) even though one-hundred and two years old, jumped for joy and called his whole family together to let them know that they were all moving back to their homeland of Yhuwdah. The Hebrews in the Temple also celebrated as they too were finally going home after nearly one-hundred and thirty years of exile. Those in his family returning were his only son Rabbi Boethus ben Ananelus with his seven sons. The seven grandsons were: Rabbi Ananelus II ben Boethus, Phabet ben Boethus, Rabbi Simon IV ben Boethus, Rabbi Joazar ben Boethus, Rabbi Sethus ben Boethus, and Rabbi Kantheras ben Boethus. The three great-grandsons through Phabet were: Rabbi Yhowshuwa III (Joshua) ben Phabet, Eliam ben Phabet, and Rabbi Ishmael I ben Phabet. Rabbi Ishmeal I had a son, great-great grandson Rabbi Gamaliel ben Ishmael I. Rabbi Yhowshuwa (Joshua) III had two daughters so the great-great-granddaughters were Yehanne (Jane) bat Yhowshuwa III and Elizabeth bat Yhowshuwa III. Thus there were seventeen members of Sadducee Rabbi Ananelus covering five generations returning to the great city of Yruwshalaim in 37 B.C.

Also, in the long caravan of camels, donkeys, oxen, and horses and among the carts and wagons piled high with family possessions was Prince Matityahu (Mattat) ben Levi with his son Prince Alexander Helios III (Heli) and his daughter Princess Alexandra III. They all began the two-hundred and eighty mile journey across the wilderness desert as two separate families but by Divine Intervention the bloodlines of the Sadducee Rabbi would unite with the Davidic Yhuwdah (Judah) Princes to forever change history. They had not traveled but two miles from the city gates of Leontopolis (Heliopolis) Mitsrayim (Egypt) when bored teenage thirteen-year old Elizabeth asked her father, Rabbi Yhowshuwa III, "Are we there yet, I don't have anything to do?" This made twenty-nine year old Prince Alexander Helios III laugh as he looked at his twenty-six year old sister. The caravan tried to travel fifty miles each day so as to compete the long and hot journey in six days to arrive in the great Yruwshalaim before Sabbath began. At each watering stop Rabbi Yhowshuwa III would visit with Prince Matityahu ben Levi about what the great city of Yruwshalaim was like. On Thursday night, the last night before the Sabbath, Rabbi Yhowshuwa III ask Prince Matityahu ben Levi what he was going to do when they arrived in the Upper City of Yruwshalaim. Prince Matityahu ben Levi let out a chuckle as he wiped the sweat off his brow and said, "The first thing I am going to do is to go find Melek'Beyth Aer (Henry Ayers), the fan maker in the Upper City and have a fan made for the house. News from Yruwshalaim has it that his twenty-six year old Yhowchanan ben Melek'Beyth Aer (John Henry Ayers) has taken over and expanded the business." Shortly before the ninth-hour prayers (3:00 P.M.) the long caravan entered the Upper City in 37 B.C. and a loud wail came from the home of Yhowchanan ben Melek 'Beyth Aer (John Henry Ayers) as his new baby son, Ya'kov (James Henry) Melek'Beyth Aer (Ayers) ben Yhowchanan Aer was making his displeasure known to the world.

13

When the heavens heard that boisterous wail of newborn Ya'kov (James) ben Yhowchanan Aer (Ayers), that little speck of pure bright light grew in intensity and began to move closer to earth. The two watchful evil minions snarled and growled and immediately headed to the evil cauldron of wickedness belonging to the dark lord, Satan. As soon as they entered into the thick black billowing smoke they began to shout, "Its coming! The light is coming!" The dark lord, rose in a fit of rage screaming, "Why is He coming? What does He want in my domain? Who does Yahuah Yahusha think He is trespassing into my world? He must be destroyed at all costs! Quick you two minions fly to all my lieutenant commanders and tell them to form a wall to cast a great shadow upon the earth. His light must not penetrate to mankind! Now go, time is wasting and the victory of death and destruction must be mine, all mine!"

Every evil demonic beast was called to stand over the territory of Yhuwdah (Judea). They lined up shoulder to shoulder and many rows in depth. They spread out their large black wings of darkness above their heads to block the pure light coming from a speck in the heavens. However, all the legions of the dark lord could not stop the speck of light as it burned the wings of those it shown upon like a laser light. As soon as others would take the place of the wounded demon, they would retreat in pain. The lieutenant commanders of the dark lord tried to control the chaos of darkness and rotated demonic beast to the speck of light as soon as possible. Their efforts were to no avail but they knew not to retreat because failure was not an option of their master, the dark lord, Satan. The speck of light continued to grow minutely larger and its power was intensified as it neared.

Herod (Hordos) the Great welcomed Sadducee Rabbi Ananelus ben Ananias and his family to the great city of Yruwshalaim. He helped them find homes in the Upper City after the Sabbath and planned an official declaration of Rabbi Ananelus as the *Gadowl Kohen,* High Priest the following week causing turmoil among the Pharisees on the Sanhedrin. However, the minority Sadducees were rejoicing because they now had the support of the political throne and the high seat of religious organization in their favor. Finally, no more persecutions from the Pharisees, no more oral traditional law from the Pharisees, no more talk of angelic beings and no more talk of being raised from the dead. They finally owned the Sanhedrin even if they were the minority.

Herod the Great had a couple of servants help one-hundred and two year old Rabbi Ananelus ben Ananias to the top steps of the Temple so the packed crowd could witness the changing of religious power to the Sadducees. Rabbi Ananelus bowed his head in respect to King Herod the Great when he had reached the top step. Then King Herod the Great presented the *begedi kohen,* garments of the priest, to Rabbi Ananelus. First, he gave him the linen *miknac,* underpants that went from the waist to the knees; second he gave him the linen *kethoneth,* undershirt; third he gave him the *m'iyl,* robe; forth, he gave him the *abnet,* sash belt; fifth, he gave him the *ephowd,* shoulder piece; sixth, he gave him the *choshen,* breastplate of twelve precious jewels; seventh, he gave him the *mitsnepheth,* turban tiara; eigth, he gave him the golden *tsiyts,* square plate, to be worn on the forehead surrounding the turban tiara with the inscription

QODESH YAHUAH, Sanctity of Yahweh; and lastly he carefully presented him with the *Uwriym and Tummiym*, Urim and Thummim stones of Truth. Rabbi Ananelus was then ushered behind the closed doors of the Temple to bath and to put on his *begedi kohen*, priestly clothes. The crowd buzzed with endless chatter in anticipation of the reappearance of Rabbi Ananelus.

When he was ready to go back outside, the Temple doors opened slowly and *showfars*, curved ram horned trumpets, began blowing. Then Herod the Great raised his arms for silence to speak as Rabbi Ananelus stood beside him, "Fellow Hebrew brothers and sisters, citizens of the great city of Yruwshalaim, people of the territory of Yhuwdah (Judea), a province of the Roman Empire." At the utterance of these last words, the crowd began to buzz in a low tone which was quickly silenced by Herod the Great and the appearance of the armed palace and temple guards. Then Herod the Great continued, "Today in the year of 37 B.C., I, King Herod Hordos the Great proudly presents to you your new *Gadowl Kohen*, High Priest, Sadducee Rabbi Ananelus ben Ananias, descendant of the priestly line of Onais and the House of Tsadowq (Zadok) descendants of Aharown (Aaron) from the tribal branch of Levi." Then the crowd sounded shrills and yelled, *"Halal Yah"*, celebrate to Yahuah (Hallelujah). It was a jubilant afternoon and the city was once again filled with celebration and joy.

The old priest, Rabbi Ananelus could not take the daily rigors of the priesthood so after a month of service, prudence compelled King Herod the Great to remove him and to fill his position with the Rabbi's son, Sadducee Rabbi Boethus ben Ananelus as *Gadowl Kohen*, High Priest. Rabbi Boethus was very knowledgeable in the Torah Law of Mosheh (Moses), however, he was a hot-head and had little tolerance of the Pharisee stance on the oral law. This created even larger divisions between the two religious parties in the Sanhedrin, which became a constant stream of complaints coming before the throne of King Herod the Great causing him great irritation. Therefore, after five months of haranguing and complaining by the Pharisees, in the early spring of 36 B.C., Herod the Great replaced Rabbi Boethus with his oldest son Rabbi Ananelus II ben Boethus, grandson of the old Rabbi Ananelus I as the new *Gadowl Kohen,* High Priest. This move pleased the Sanhedrin because Rabbi Ananelus II was mild-mannered, more tolerant and was not as opinionated as his father, Rabbi Boethus.

The atmosphere of peace finally seemed to reach the Sanhedrin and the Temple. The next day after Saducee Rabbi Ananelus II was appointed *Gadowl Kohen,* High Priest, he had to present an offering in the Most Sacred Place on the altar and stand before the Arc of the Covenant. Due to such a quick turnover of the office of the *Gadowl Kohen,* High Priest, the *miknac,* underpants, did not fit because his grandfather and father were a lot larger in the waist than him. He tried to tighten the *abnet,* sash belt, as tight as he could but they still fell down to his ankles. Finally, the third-hour (9:00 a.m.) prayers were about to begin so he just kicked them aside and finished getting dressed and hurried to the altar. He took three steps inside the Most Sacred Place and Yahuah Yahusha stuck him dead. The attending *kohen,* heard the thud and pulled on the rope but the bells did not jingle that were on the bottom of the *m'iyl,* robe. Therefore, they pulled harder on the rope until the dead body of Sadducee Rabbi Ananelus II ben Boethus was pulled through the curtain. Then they tore their robes and began to wail with great lamentation. The whole Temple became somber and word soon reached the palace.

King Herod the Great was beside himself with the drama surrounding the Temple *Gadowl Kohen,* High Priest. Therefore, he summoned his seventeen year-old brother-in-law Aristobulus III Maccabim, the younger brother of his second wife Mariamne I, to enlighten him on what just happened in the Temple. King Herod the Great said, "Young Maccabim, please explain to me what just happened in the Temple with High Priest Rabbi Ananelus II. I must account to Rome what is happening concerning not finding a worthy *Gadowl Kohen*, High Priest." Aristobulus III, the last male (Hasmonean) Maccabim alive except for his great-uncle who was in exile in Babylon, the son of Alexander and Alexandra II, replied, "His Excellency Herod the Great, I have heard from the Sanhedrin members that Rabbi Ananelus II did not present himself in the Most Sacred Place wearing all the *begedi kohen*, clothing of the priest. Specifically, he was without the *miknac*, underpants because the ones of his grandfather and father were too big and fell off. There is a warning in our Torah Law in the book of 'Elleh Shem (Exodus) in the twenty-eighth chapter the last two verses. It states, *'Make for them linen pants to cover to secrecy by hiding their body flesh of their sexual body parts. They will exist from the waist as far as the thighs. The will come to pass to be on Aharown (Aaron) and on his sons in their going into the tent for the appointment at the place of meeting or in their coming near to the altar to attend as a worshipper in the Sacred Place, so they will not lift and carry the perversity and evil and die! It is an eternal statute to him and to his seed after him."* King Herod the Great cupped his chin with his right hand, looked the young Maccabim up and down and said, "Young brother-in-law, you seem to know the Torah Law and have a family history of upholding it. You are now the new *Gadowl Kohen*." This pleased the Pharisees since Aristobulus III Maccabim leaned towards their religious stances.

    Pharisee Aristobulus III Maccabim was a good *Gadowl Kohen*, High Priest, and for a whole year kept the peace in the Sanhedrin.

However, his political opinions caused paranoia with his brother-in-law the king on more than one occasion at lavish banquets and royal gatherings. He used his powerful and privileged position to bend the ear of the king especially to return his great-uncle Hyrcanus II from Babylon to prevent him from encouraging the Parthians (Persia-modern Iran) from waging war on the great city of Yruwshalaim (Jerusalem) and his throne. Therefore, in 36 B.C. King Herod the Great invited the former High Priest to return to the great city of Yruwshalaim. Hyrcanus II Maccabim accepted and Herod received him with every mark of respect, ignoring the deformity of no ears and assigned to him the first place at his table and the presidency of the state council. The paranoia of Herod the Great did not diminish but increased so in the early year of 35 B.C. he held a lavish pool party at his palace and drowned his young brother-in-law *Gadowl Kohen*, High Priest, Aristobulus III Maccabim, the last Hasmonean High Priest.

King Herod the Great looked once again the next day to the Onais Dynasty that had returned from Mitsrayim (Egypt) to fill the vacant temple position. Therefore, he chose the next in line from the family of the Sadducee Rabbbi Boethus ben Ananelus I. The next in line was his second son, Rabbi Yhowshuwa (Joshua) III, who unknown to King Herod the Great had the invisible protective hand of Yahuah Yahusha on his family. Rabbi Yhowshuwa III was rising in power within the Pharisee party because he differed with his Sadducee family members over the validity of the oral law. So, Pharisee Rabbi Yhowshuwa III ran home to tell his wife the great news of his new position within the Sanhedrin and prestige from the throne of the palace. As soon as he opened the door to his house, his two beautiful daughters with long black hair embraced him. Yehanne (Jane) now seventeen years old and Elizabeth now fifteen years old said to their mother, *"Ab beyth"*, Father's home. Yhowshuwa III then gathered his family to tell them the news.

"I have some grand news to share with you. Yahuah Yahusha has smiled upon our family today and your eyes are now looking at the new *Gadowl Kohen*, High Priest of the Temple in the great city of Yruwshalaim (Jerusalem)," explained Yhowshuwa III. His wife said, "*Halal Yah!* Hallelujah honey you deserve it because you have worked so hard to be His servant. However, you are not the only one with news today, right girls?" Both daughters chimed in at the same time, "That's right, we have a surprise too." Then they put their hands over their mouths and began giggling. Puzzled Yhowshuwa III threw his arms in the air and said, "Ok, I surrender what could be more surprising than me becoming *HaGadowl Kohen*, the High Priest?" Then his wife stood square in front of him and put her hand on his shoulder trying not to be excited and said teasingly, "Well… you see…uh….there was….today….." "Spit it out woman, do you want to tell me or not," chided Yhowshuwa III. The two girls broke out in loud laughter, loving to see their father squirm and blurted, "Come on mom quit teasing father and tell him. We don't want the new *Gadowl Kohen*, High Priest, to use his power and ask Yahuah to call down lightning bolts do we?" "Very funny, very funny, the whole family is a bunch of court jesters, eh?" joked Yhowshuwa (Joshua) III.

After the laughter calmed down, his wife continued, "Today there was a knock on the door, and the wealthy rug merchant, Yehowram (meaning Yahuah raised) was standing there. I thought maybe you were going to surprise me and get a new area rug for the conversation room. However, to my embarrassment of thinking I was getting a new rug, knowing full well all along that you pinched your *leptons* (pennies), he assured me that was not the reason why he was here. After all he did request to see you and not me. So, I told him that you were still speaking at the Sanhedrin. He requested that you contact him soon because he wants to start negotiating the hand of our daughter Yehanne (Jane) in marriage to his oldest son, Yehowyaqim (meaning Yahuah will raise). His son will soon be taking over the business and maybe I will get my new area rug after all." "Well, I'll be. A rug merchant in our family, eh?" stated the surprised Yhowshuwa III. Then he bear-hugged his oldest daughter and swung her around a couple of times. "Mama, that's not all! Tell him the rest of the story," demanded the younger Elysheba (Elizabeth) meaning (oath of Yahuah), with her hands on both of her hips and her lower lip stuck out.

"You mean that there is more good news?" said the joyful *Gadowl Kohen*, High Priest. Then his wife put her arm around the shoulders of Elysheba and answered, "Oh yes, there is more. Not long after Yehowram left, I was visited by the Sanhedrin scribe, Pharisee Rabbi Zeker, meaning (remember). He said that you had been summoned to the Palace by King Herod the Great and that he wanted to visit with you today." "What does he know on the Sanhedrin that I don't know?" quipped Yhowshuwa III. Then his wife put her finger to her lips quickly as a gesture for him to keep quiet and continued, "The visit was not for Temple business but personal. He also wants to visit with you about giving the hand of Elysheba in marriage to his son, young Pharisee Rabbi Zkaryah, meaning (Yahuah has remembered). A shocked Yhowshuwa III stood there frozen and speechless and finally said as if dazed, "A double wedding? Both of my beautiful rose buds plucked in one day? I am so happy but I am not ready for an empty nest, mama bird." Then his wife said, "Ok, girls both of you go stand on each side of your father because I have more good news to share with all of you." Yehanne (Jane) and Elysheba

(Elizabeth) furrowed their eye brows with deep puzzled looks but obeyed their mother. The wife of Yhowshuwa III took a deep breath and as her eyes moistened she explained, "Well, papa bird, you don't have to have an empty nest because mama bird has laid an egg and is hatching a new chick to be born by the end of this year." The mouth of Yhowshuwa III gapped wide open and stammered, "Wha......" Then the overwhelmed new *Gadowl Kohen*, High Priest fell over like a towering cedar tree and crashed to the floor.

By the end of the week before the Sabbath, the *erusin*, betrothal for each girl was finalized with each *mohar*, dowry set and they were considered married. Yehowyaquim gave Yeanne (Jane) a gold ring as her green eyes sparkled like diamonds and then Zkaryah gave Elysheba her gold ring and she let out a little giggle. Then proud father, Rabbi Yhowshuwa III said a blessing over each couple with joyful tears streaming down his cheeks into his beard. Now the girls were forbidden to other young men who might come calling as they awaited the second stage of the marriage. For now they were to remain under their father's house until the actual wedding ceremony. The double *nesuin*, second stage of the marriage and actual wedding ceremony was set two days following the Feast of Tabernacles in the fall giving each groom plenty of time to pay in full the *mohar*, dowry. The great city of Yruwshalaim was all abuzz since this was the first double wedding since before the "Maccabim Revolt" one-hundred and thirty-two years ago. The market place sounded like gaggling geese since the women gossips had plenty to chatter about. These three prominent families were now under the ever watchful spyglass of these cut-throat barracudas feeding on every movement and word spoken by them.

Finally, the big day for the *nesuin*, wedding ceremony came. It was a beautiful fall day with a vast blue cloudless sky overhead and the air crisp with the promise of winter rains next new moon (month). The families, relatives, invited guests, and nosey onlookers all gathered at the town square in the Upper City. The double *chuppah*, was set up. The *chuppah* represented a Hebrew home symbolized by a white cloth sheet canopy with the sheet's four corners wrapped around four poles. Just as a *chuppah* is open on all four sides, so was the tent of Abraham open for hospitality. Thus, the *chuppah* represented hospitality to one's guests. This humble "home" initially lacks furniture as a reminder that the basis of a Hebrew home is the people within it, not the material possessions. In a spiritual sense, the covering of the *chuppah* represented the presence of Yahuah over the covenant of the marriage. The *chuppah* used for the *nesuin*, wedding ceremony, on this day was trimmed on the edges with dark blue trimmings and tassels hanging from the edges to represent the prayer shawl of the grooms.

Just before Yehowyaqim went under the *chuppah* he covered Yehanne's (Jane) face with her *hinuma*, veil and asked her permission to enter the *chuppah* representing that he was asking her permission to become her provider, protector and procreator. Yehanne (Jane) replied, "*Ken*, Yes." Then Zkaryah covered the face of Elysheba with her *hinuma*, veil and asked her permission to enter the *chuppah*. She smiled under the *hinuma*, veil and said, "*Ken*, Yes." So Zkaryah went under the *chuppah* and stood next to Yehowyaqim. Now both young men have represented headship and ownership of the home on behalf of their future families and publicly demonstrated their new responsibilities towards their wives. Then Yehanne (Jane) and Elysheba (Elizabeth) entered the *chuppah*, faced their husbands and took a hold of both of their hands. Next, the *ketubah*, the one-way contract agreement of the groom containing the agreement for protection for the wife, the price to be paid to the wife in case of a divorce and the promise of providing clothing, food and conjugal relations was read for each groom.

Then each groom was given a chance to speak personally to each bride. Yehowyaqim was first to speak to his bride Yehanne (Jane), "My dearest wife, Yehanne, as I look deeply into your lovely eyes, I must tell you that Yahuah has given me a gift more valuable than a precious jewel to treasure for eternity. You are to me like a beautiful flower garden. Your scent is like a garden of aromatic roses surrounded by lilacs and lavender. Your beauty is like Yahuah painting a breathtaking sunset full of blues, purples, pinks and oranges. As you hold my hands with your ever so tender touch, I am bound to you and you to me united as one. As Yahuah as my witness I shall always cherish you more than even my own life. I will not surrender my last breath in my effort to save and protect you. You are my lily of the valley and my rose of Sharon for the rest of my grateful life."

Next, young Rabbi Zkaryah cleared his throat and then focused on Elysheba (Elizabeth), "My spunky and beautiful bride, Elysheba, as you embrace my hands I am reminded of the comfort found in the Torah Law. As the Torah Law is made up of the letters of the *Otiyot Yeshod,* alphabet, which is circular and never ending, I can't speak of the joy that you bring to me because the words are so many that all the papyrus grass in world could not contain my feelings for you. Just as Yahuah has written about His unending love for us in His Torah, I am humbled that you will allow me to write my unending love for you upon your tender heart. Yahuah can't break His promises in the Torah and I will never break my promise to always love and cherish only you as we will grow old together. Yes, Elysheba your are the 'Oath of Yahuah' and it is my oath with Yahuah our Creator as our witness, that I will spend every moment of the rest of my life to protect and provide for you according to only His standards and

His Torah Law. May every laugh that we laugh together be founded upon His joy; may every tear that we share together flow into rivers of hope and peace instead of despair; may the unending love that we share together grow deeper than the depths of heaven each passing day and may each sunset that we share together for the rest of our lives be strengthened knowing that Yahuah will always provide a pre-dawn light."

Gadowl Kohen, High Priest Rabbi Yhowshuwa III wiped the tears from his eyes as he was moved at the deep love and lifetime commitment of his son-in-laws for his daughters and then prepared to give the *sheva brachot*, seven blessings over the grooms and the brides. He raised both his arms towards heaven and said,

"*Barukh atah Yahuah Yah melekh ha-olam, bo'rei p'ri hagafen*. Blessed are You, Yahuah, our Yah, sovereign of the universe, Who creates the fruit of the vine."

"*Barukh atah Yahuah Yah melech ha-olam shehakol bara lichvodo*. Blessed are You, Yahuah, our Yah, sovereign of the universe, Who created everything for Your Glory." This blessing was to reflect both grace to accept what one can't change and recognition that everyone has unique and irreplaceable talents as keys to a harmonious marriage.

"*Barukh atah Yahuah Yah melekh ha-olam, yotzer haa'dam*. Blessed are You, Yahuah, our Yah, sovereign of the universe, Who creates red-fleshed human beings."

"*Barukh atah Yahuah Yah melekh ha-olam, asher yatzar et ha-adam b'tzalmo, b'tzelem d'mut tavnito, v'hitkin lo mimenu binyan adei ad. Baruch atah Yahuah, yotzeir ha-adam*. Blessed are You, Yahuah, our Yah, sovereign of the universe, Who creates red-fleshed human beings in Your image, fashioning perpetuated life. Blessed are You, Yahuah, creator of red-fleshed human beings."

"*Sos tasis y'tageil ha-akara b'kibutz baneha l'tocha b'simcha. Baruch atah Yahuah, m'sameach Tzion b'vaneha.* May the baron one exult and be glad as her children are joyfully gathered to her. Blessed are You, Yahuah, Who gladden Zion with her children."

"*Sameiach tesamach reiim ha-ahuvim k'sameichacha y'tzircha b'gan eden mikedem. Baruch atah Yahuah m'sameiach chatan v'chalah.* Great perfect joy to these loving companions, as You did Your creations in the Garden of Eden. Blessed are You, Yahuah, Who grants the joy of groom and bride."

"*Baruch atah Yahuah Yah melech ha-olam, asher bara sason v'simcha chatan v'kallah, gilah rinah ditzah v'chedvah, ahavah v'achavah v'shalom v'reut. M'hera Yahuah Yah yishammah b'arei Yhudah uv-chutzot Y'rushalayim kol sason v'kol simcha, kol chatan v'kol kalah, kol mitzhalot chatanim meichupatam u-n'arim mimishte n'ginatam. Baruch atah Adonai, m'sameiach chatan im hakalah.* Blessed are You, Yahuah, our Yah, sovereign of the universe, Who created joy and gladness, groom and bride, mirth, song, delight and rejoicing, love and harmony and peace and companionship. Yahuah our Yah, may there ever be heard in the cities of Judah and in the streets of Jerusalem voices of joy and gladness, voices of groom and bride, the jubilant voices of those joined in marriage under the bridal canopy, the voices of young people feasting and singing. Blessed are You, Yahuah, Who causes the groom to rejoice with his bride."

Then Rabbi Yhowshuwa III smiled at each of his daughters and gave each one of them a gentle kiss on their foreheads and presented the new couples to the onlookers who were now making loud shrills and shouting encouragement. Then the wedding celebration moved up the street to the vast grounds of the rug merchant, Zeker. The air was filled with celebration of musical instruments, laughter and the smell of table upon table of food prepared for the wedding supper. Yruwshalaim (Jerusalem) was once again the 'City of Peace' filled with fun, family and fellowship. In mid-December of that year, 35 B.C. little Chana (Hannah) was born and Pharisee Rabbi Yhowshuwa III the *Gadowl Kohen*, High Priest strutted around like a proud peacock.

All the joy and celebration in the great city of Yruwshalaim increased the speed of that spot of light traveling through the darkness of the heavens towards that wall of dark demonic beasts and ultimately the earth. Each time an evil beast was wounded the lieutenant commanders would replace it with another one. The rotation of injured beasts and fresh ones became more frequent as the light got nearer because it burned more intense into the flesh of the screaming beasts. Some howled and tumbled out of the way while others simply fell in a heap where they were stepped on by their unwilling replacements. The hoards of wickedness were powerless to stop this Light of the world from Yahuah. The lieutenant commanders knew that they could not let this coming pre-dawn Light hit the earth and become the Sunrise on High. Therefore, their vocal screams and hissing demanded total obedience from their nervous troops of evil minions. The commands were hard to distinguish over the scowling whimpers and deep hollow moaning of the never-ending wounded demonic beings. The long sharp talons of the lieutenant commanders would lash out at the flesh of hesitant recruits who were unwilling to use any part of their bodies to form a dark wall to stop the light from reaching the earth. Also, the joyful praises from the earth to Yahuah Yahusha hurt the eardrums of the wicked minions of the dark lord, Satan.

14

For four years the black wickedness tried to form a wall to prevent the pure light from Heaven to reach the earth. The wounded beasts with burns on their wings and bodies where the pure light touched them burned with intense pain. The lieutenant commanders had to fight harder to keep their ranks of dark legions in order. Finally two of the lieutenant commanders in 31 B.C. ordered their legions to charge and attack the light because it continued to travel ever so closer towards reaching the earth. The evil minions hesitantly obeyed and charged the pure light in full force. However, when the dark minions of wickedness were fully exposed to the pure light, they burst into flames and fell towards the earth in a colossal flaming heap impacting with great force near the great city of Yruwshalaim (Jerusalem) in the territory of Yhuwdah (Judah). Their charred bodies exploded on impact and the debris from their filth filled the air and a blast of wind with great force headed towards the great city of Yruwshalaim and the Hebrew people.

Little three and a half year old Chana (Hanna) gripped her mother's hand securely as they traveled to the market with their next door neighbors six-year old Ya'kov (James) Aer (Ayers) and his mother. Ya'kov glanced over to Chana and said, "I don't have to hold my mother's hand because I am grown-up, six years old now." Chana stuck out her lower lip and replied, "So!" The two mothers rolled their eyes and headed to the bakers and then on down to the fresh produce market in the Lower City. Just as they passed the meat market the wind began to blow and the hanging meat began to sway. The items of the coppersmith down the street began to clang against each other making the sound like a booth of wind chimes. Then the wind became really strong blowing over tables and the ground beneath them began to tremor. As merchants tried to protect their wares the tremors turned into violent shaking. Ya'kov (James) cried out and grabbed his mother's hand and little Chana began to cry in fear. Then the kiosks began to tumble into the streets with all the merchandise, animals began to get loose and run up and down the streets without their owners. Panic was on the people's faces as they scrambled to safety. The mothers held tightly to their children to keep them from being trampled by the panicked crowd and scared animals. Then stone houses and shops began to crumble and stones fell into the streets, cries for help and screams filled the air along with the roaring from the shaking and the big gust of wind. For what seemed like an eternity was over in a few minutes. The howling wind had ceased and the ground was once again stable. Then braying of an ownerless donkey could be heard down the street along with the moaning and groaning of several spice merchant camels who had strung their cargo all along the street.

The two mothers brushed the fine earthquake dust off their clothes and their *mitpachats*, head scarves, and quickly gathered their two little children and headed back home to the Upper City. Little Chana (Hanna) and Ya'kov (James) were drug, prodded and pushed through all the debris which made quite an obstacle course for the two women trying to get home as fast as possible. Chana followed her mother's commands while little Ya'kov when not being coaxed by his mother would stand and gaze in amazement or ask to stop and explore a particular damaged site. If that didn't get her attention then he would ask a million questions without taking a breath. Finally his mother had enough, stopped, put her hands on her hips, looked him squarely in the eye and in exasperation said, "Honestly, child. Do you have to be so inquisitive? If you say one more word before we get home, your father will have your backside. Do you understand?" Three year old Chana (Hanna) giggled and then received a stern look and a shaking of the index finger from her mother. Then six year old Ya'kov (James) said, *"Ken em." "Yes, mother."* Just as she began to turn around he continued, *"Em,* Mother, when you were so scared as the ground was shaking and you held me tight and told me that you loved me, did I do a good job of being your little man and protect you?" She said, *"Ken,* yes." Then he put his little hands on his little hips and with great confidence asked, "Do you still love me as much now as you did then." His mother answered, *"Ken,* yes, but we need to hurry home and *halak,* walk." Then Ya'kov looked straight at Chana (Hanna) and said grinning from ear to ear, "Ok, but since I am grown up, six years old, I am big enough to lead you home safely. Are you all ready to follow me?" At that, the two mothers smiled at each other and quietly muttered, "Out of the mouth of babes." Little Ya'kov led them home as fast as his two little legs could walk and even jogged ahead.

The great city of Yruwshalaim (Jerusalem) suffered considerable damage in the earthquake and spent the next twelve months repairing the destruction. After the earthquake King Herod the Great in 30 B.C. was more and more paranoid. First, he charged Hyrcanus II Maccabim with plotting with the Nabateans (Arabs) to overthrow his thrown so he put him to death. Then he accused his favorite wife Mariamne I Maccabim, the granddaughter of Hyrcanus II Maccabim, of plotting to kill him. Therefore, when she learned of this she feared for her life and was so tired of his paranoia that she quit sleeping with the king.

Paranoia was not just on the throne in Yruwshalaim but it was also prevalent on the throne in Rome. Caesar Octavian Augustus was still livid over General Marcus Antonius divorcing his sister and marrying Queen Cleopatra of Mitsrayim (Egypt). Octavian's anger spilled over to paranoia as he now believed that General Marcus in Antioch, Syria was going to join forces with Queen Cleopatra in Alexandria, Mitsrayim (Egypt) and invade Rome and take away his throne and position as *Divi Filius*, son of a god. Therefore, that same year in 30 B.C. he gathered all his troops in Rome and crossed the Mediterranean Sea with a great navy to invade Alexandria, Mitsrayim. They arrived on the great Nile River Delta and then marched full force to siege the capital city of Mitsrayim (Egypt). Queen Cleopatra received a warning about Caesar Octavian's invasion and began to defend the city with her army and also sent word to Antioch, Syria requesting help from her husband Marcus Antonius. He gathered his powerful Syrian army of Roman legions and crossed the Mediterranean Sea around the Island of Cyprus and headed to the port city of Alexandria, Mitsrayim (Egypt) to give aid to the Egyptian army and Queen Cleopatra against the Roman invasion of his ex-brother-in-law Caesar Octavian Augustus.

Caesar Augustus and some of his troops broke through the barrier and entered the palace of Queen Cleopatra. When she had received the warning previously she hid her three children that she and General Marcus Antonius had together, two sons and a daughter named Cleopatra Selene. However, her son Caesarion that she had with Caesar Julius Caesar was now fourteen years old and refused to leave his mother's side by her throne. The outnumbered palace guards were no match for the Roman soldiers of Caesar Augustus so they were able to break through the great wooden doors of the Great Throne Room of Pharaoh's. Two body guards of Augustus seized young Caesarion and brought him to Augustus as Queen Cleopatra was held captive on her throne, helplessly watching. Caesar Octavian Augustus drew his sword from his scabbard and said to young Caesarion, "I am the only *Divi Filius*, son of a god, of Rome." Then he thrust his sword through the mid-section of fourteen year old Caesarion until the blade was exposed through his back. He pulled the sword out of the son of Julius Caesar and the teenage boy fell to the floor bleeding profusely. Then a Roman Centurion came running through the great throne room doors and said, "Hail, Caesar. We need you on the battlefield immediately because Marcus Antonius has come from Syria with his powerful legions and are attacking and penetrating our rear flanks."

At that news, Caesar Augustus spun around and commanded, "Guard these door and do not let her escape." So the two guards who were restraining Queen Cleopatra released her and posted themselves at the great throne room doors. Cleopatra ran to her bleeding and dying son and held his bloody body near hers, rocking him back and forth as if he was a young toddler again. With rivers of tears flowing from her painted eyes she tried to comfort her dying son. Then he looked up at her with glazed eyes and with gasping breath and painful agony said, *"Di...vi...F...il...us? Son of a god?"* Queen Cleopatra replied with an aching heart, "Yes, my son, you are *Divi Filus."* Then the only son of Julius Caesar fell limp in her bloody arms as she buried her face into his neck and sobbed bitter tears. She removed her blood stained blue silk cape and put it over his dead body and went back to a private dressing room just off the great hall to change clothes for when Marcus Antonius would come and rescue her. However she could not escape because the only way out now was the through the throne room doors which now were heavily guarded by the soldiers of Caesar Augustus because all other doors had been sealed off. She could not even get a message to or from outside those four walls that were now a prison cell.

General Marcus Antonius and his army fought valiantly and formed a penetrating wedge directly in the center of the troops of Caesar Augustus. Roman soldiers were fighting Roman soldiers with some of the more inexperienced soldiers of the Caesar defecting to the more experienced and better trained legions of General Marcus Antonius. As the wedge of General Marcus Antonius began penetrating at will through the center of the main force of Caesar Augustus, Caesar began rallying his troops on the right and left flanks to support and stop the wedge of General Marcus. The Mitsrayim (Egyptian) soldiers were also trying to rally to the center wedge of General Marcus. The hand to hand combat was fierce as sword clashed against sword as it was difficult to tell which Roman soldiers belonged to which commander. The centurions of Caesar Augustus began to get confused because they could no longer fully recognize their own troops from those of General Marcus.

Then Caesar Octavian Augustus pulled fifty soldiers from battle and had them to start burning the entire city of Alexandria. As the set fires began to blaze, citizens and wounded soldiers of Queen Cleopatra tried to escape the flames only to find Roman soldiers in the streets to slaughter them. Men, women and children of all ages were cut to the ground by wielding Roman swords stained with innocent blood. Many were trapped in homes and buildings as they caught fire as the flames freely skipped from one building to another making the city an inferno out of control. Thick black billowing smoke filled the air and the heat from the flames became unbearable. Agonizing screams of trapped humans echoed in the streets as human flesh was being consumed by flames of fire. Animals began to stampede wildly in the streets trying to escape the consuming flames adding confusion to a helpless city already in overwhelming panic. The soldiers of all three armies could hardly fight as they chocked on the fumes of the thick billowing smoke and their eyes were filled with blurred vision. With the interior of Alexandria's walls being consumed by fire, Caesar Octavian Augustus changed his military strategy and ordered his split right and left flanks to give up their side positions and rally directly behind the troops of General Marcus Antonius allowing his army to penetrate into the interior of the burning city. This would leave the army of the General trapped with blazing flames in front and Octavian's lesser experienced army at the rear.

General Marcus Antonius recognized what Caesar Augustus was trying to do so he 'out foxed' the 'old fox'. He left his commanders in charge of the army to remain outside the gates as a ploy to give General Marcus time to get Queen Cleopatra and their children to safety. While his seasoned army fought off their Roman countrymen, he took fifty of his trained assassins inside the walls of the burning city of Alexandria and headed straight to the palace. One by one his assassins eliminated the lookout guards and traps left behind by Caesar Augustus. General Marcus knew he had to move quickly without delay because his troops would not be able to hold off their Roman countrymen for very long. As they moved swiftly along the smoke and flame filled streets towards the palace all he could think about was to save his wife and children whom he loved more than life itself. They would have to escape deep into Africa because he knew that Caesar Octavian Augustus would hunt them down like game animals. He also knew that his troops of loyal Roman soldiers would be executed by being impaled on wooden cross for treason, but they were willing to die for their General.

Finally, they reached the palace doors, eliminating the guards and then proceeded directly to the Throne Room of the Pharaoh's where he should find his wife, the Queen. They burst through the wooden doors, and his soldier assassins remained outside to stand guard but his four personal body guards entered the great hall with him. To his astonishment he was not met with open arms of his wife running towards him. Instead the room was completely empty except a small lump of a figure covered by a blue silk cape on the floor near the throne platform. He recognized the bloodied silk cape as that of Queen Cleopatra so he removed it from the small frame that lay lifeless on the royal floor. When he saw who it was, he cried out, "Oh no, little cousin Caesarion! What has Augustus done to you and your mother?" General Marcus Antonius sent his four body guards to search the room and its adjoining private chambers. Then he assumed that the blood on the blue silk cape was that of the Queen so he continued to cry out, "I can't live without you Cleopatra and our children." With part of the palace now on fire, he knew it was over. Therefore, he took his sword and thrust it into his own midsection committing suicide. He fell next to his step-son and died.

Not long after this, one of the body guards returned with Queen Cleopatra and their three little children safe and sound. She saw the body of Marcus hovered over the body of Caesarion and thought he was just grieving for his cousin and step-son from Julius Caesar but when she approached near the two bodies she realized that he too was dead. She screamed, "No, not you, my General and husband!" Then she staggered to her throne and collapsed into its massive seat. She wept bitterly and cried out in agonizing grief. One of the body guards of General Marcus said to her, "Hurry, my Queen we must get out of here!" She replied, "Make sure the hall is clear for the safety of the children and ourselves." As the body guards checked with the posted assassin soldiers on the outside of the doors, Queen Cleopatra opened a hidden compartment in the broad arms of the throne. She removed a long narrow box from the compartment and then placed her hand carefully into the box trying to keep the lid closed as much as possible. Then she winced, dropped the box and slumped to the floor crawling on her hands and knees to the side of Marcus Antonius and young Caesarion. After the long and narrow box fell to the floor, a very poisonous horned viper asp crawled from its box of captivity and slithered behind the throne. Cleopatra grew very sleepy and then died next to the other two lifeless bodies.

The body guards saw what had happened and quickly ran through the streets outside of the palace announcing that General Marcus Antonius and Queen Cleopatra were dead. When the news reached the ranks of his troops they surrendered and laid down their weapons. Caesar Octavian Augustus quickly rode his stallion through the smoke and flames to the palace to witness personally the shallow victory. He ordered his soldiers to seize the three children of Marcus Antonius and Queen Cleopatra and put them aboard his ship to take back to Rome for his victory parade. They were placed in shackles and thrown into the bottom of the ship. The following week he led the victory parade for the celebratory crowds of Roman citizens with a great display of pomp and power. The three children ages, seven, five and three were placed in golden chains that were so heavy they could not walk. After the parade the two sons of Marcus Antonius subsequently died of torture, starvation and dehydration. However, the three-year old daughter Cleopatra Selene was spared and when she grew older was given into marriage to Juba II, the Roman client king of the territories of Numidia and Mauretania (modern day Algeria and Libya, Africa). The Roman Senate in 30 B.C. supported Caesar Octavian Augustus in annexing the territory of Mitsrayim, (Egypt) into the Roman Empire even rebuilding the burnt city of Alexandria as a major foreign seaport for the resource supply of their much demanded wheat and other grains. The gluttonous belly of the Vulture of Death was satiated with human flesh as it lifted off with its massive black wings of darkness taking its blood-thirsty long talons and its razor sharp beak towards the territory of Yhuwdah (Judea). Could King Herod the Great be the next royal figure to fall prey to this ravenous bird?

Back in the territory of Yhuwdah (Judea) as the Roman tragedy was being played out in Mitsrayim (Egypt) and Rome, *Gadowl Kohen*, High Priest, Yhowshuwa III decided to hold a great banquet to focus on other things besides the evilness of palace business and the politics of Rome. He made sure next door neighbor the fan maker Melek'Beyth (Henry) Aer (Ayers) and his son Yhowchanan Melek'Beyth (John Henry) Aer (Ayers) were invited along with his old traveling companion and friend from Mitsrayim (Egypt), Prince Matityahu ben Levi. Prince Matityahu ben Levi and his thirty-six year old bachelor son Prince Alexander III Helios even volunteered to provide all the wine for the festive banquet. Pharisee Rabbi Yhowshuwa III also was going to attempt to play 'matchmaker' for Prince Matityahu ben Levi's bachelor son at this grand banquet since his sister, the young Davidic and Maccabim Princess Alexandra III had three years ago married Ptolomee Bar Mennius, a Babylonian Exilarch who was in charge of all the Hebrew exiles living in the territory of Babylon. The *Gadowl Kohen*, High Priest was going to try to match this middle-aged Davidic Prince with a very wealthy widow from the village of Ha-ramathayim or as the Hebrews called it Ramah for short and the Greeks and Romans called it Arimathea. The village of Arimathea was located eight miles straight north of Yruwshalaim (Jerusalem) in the hills. The widow's name was Rachel and she owned many ancestral estates. She also had three teenage children from her previous marriage Yhowshuwa (Joshua),

Yownathan (Jonathan) and Yochana (JoAnna). She was in the great city of Yruwshalaim (Jerusalem) to file papers for new land acquisitions. Her former husband had been a large financial supporter of the Temple and a backer of the Pharisee causes.

The banquet hall was decorated and the five harpists were ready to play their soothing harps and provide tranquil music for the relaxing banquet. Aromas of barbecued beef over cedar and hickory wood and roasted lamb with garlic and onions filled the air as guests began to arrive. Servants began carrying in heaped platters of sweet figs, fresh melons, enormas grape clusters and large baskets of oranges, apples and pomegranates. More servants entered carrying smaller platters of roasted almonds, cashews and macadamia nuts followed by yellow cheese rounds, white cheese blocks, and bowls of curds and whey. The final items to be brought to the reclining tables were baskets of fresh baked *lechem*, bread. Some baskets were filled with twisted loaves of sweet bread while other baskets were full of raison cakes, round sour bread and even wafer type crispy fried bread served with fresh sticky-gummy syrup of honey. Of course it was not a grand banquet without the fine wine from the vineyards of the little village of Modi'im located on the main highway leading to the port city of Yofa (Joppa).

The invited guests were seated according to their pre-designated positions directly under two of the large feathered fans made by fan maker Melek'Beyth (Henry) Aer (Ayers) and his son Yhowchanan Melek'Beyth (John Henry) Aer (Ayers). The conversations around the table were kept as light as the breeze of the fans and away from politics and rumors of the palace. Even some of the powerful Sadducees seemed to be enjoying the lavish banquet provided by the host *Gadowl Kohen*, High Priest, Pharisee Rabbi Yhowshuwa III. All was going very well except Rachel of Arimathea seemed to be having more conversations with Prince Matityahu ben Levi than with his bachelor son Prince Alexander III Helios. Wealthy widow Rachel and Prince Matityahu engaged in business conversations such as contract negotiations, tax liability issues due to the throne of Herod the Great and oversight of many employees and slaves. Bachelor Prince 'Heli' thanked his gracious host and excused himself to leave early after everyone was done eating and the only thing left was grandiose bragging and empting the skin flasks of precious fine wine. The 'matchmaker' *kohen*, priest, did make a successful match but to his much surprise it was not the one that he had intended. The father of the prince took the bait not the son.

Prince Alexander III Helios stood outside in the courtyard and gazed into the night sky at the thousands of blinking lights on the canvass of a black sky and silently prayed, "*Oh Yahuah. I know that I am a Davidic Prince from the bloodline of King David and Yhuwdah (Judah) from one of the twelve tribes of Yisra'Yah (Israel) but also I am simply Eliy ben Matityahu. I do not want to rule on a throne but I want to do Your will while just simply being a husband and father. Yet you have denied me my only wish in life. Do you have a wife for me in the entire of Yhuwdah (Judea)? If so what is she like and will she simply accept a position of just queen of my household? Oh, Creator the world is such a mess and I do not want my children to have to rule with such hatred, greed, murder and lust for self-serving power. Let one of my grandchildren rule from Your throne in Tsiyown (Zion) but as for me and my family, if You have one for me, just let us live in peace away from this conflict. If you have a soul mate chosen for me then I pray that tonight You let her know with security in her heart how much I deeply love her and yearn with all my might that we be united.*" The Prince did not know that listening from a window above him was little star-eyed and beautiful five-year old Chana (Hannah).

15

The Vulture of Death arrived from Rome and with its large black outstretched wings circled over the great city of Yruwshalalim (Jerusalem) searching for its next prey. Its long blood-thirsty talons yearned to sink into the carnage of human flesh caused by deceit, murder and lust for power. However, much to the disappointment of its razor sharp beak the only activity it could see in the great city of Yruwshalaim in 29 B.C. was a joyful wedding and celebration of Prince Matityahu ben Levi and Rachel of Arimathea. Matityahu moved out of his large house in the Upper City of the great city of Yruwshalaim and turned over his Yruwshalaim estate to his bachelor son Prince Alexander III Helios. He took his new bride and teenage children back to Haramathayim (Ramah) also known as Arimathea, to help manage the sprawling ancestral estates of Rachel. The families of Pharisee Rabbi Yhowshuwa III (Joshua) and the fan-maker Melek'Beyth (Henry) Aer (Ayers) waved good-bye to their friend and neighbor as he began the second journey of his life.

A few days later, as the legions of the dark lord, Satan continued to attempt to prevent the growing ball of pure light from shining on the earth, two of the lieutenant commanders, one named Paraneumos (Abnormal Spirits) and the second Homicideium (Murders) attacked Herod the Great with their poisonous venom stinging him directly behind his ears. The next day King Herod the Great was ranting and raving in the throne room, throwing wine goblets, turning over furniture and cursing anyone and anything within his eyesight. He became literally a paranoid lunatic seeing and hearing things that never happened and made up things and believed them to be reality. He could not be reasoned with because reasoning just irritated him that much more. When he had company he screamed to be alone and when he was alone he screamed for company. He would demand food accusing his Master of the House that he was trying to starve him to death and when the food would arrive he then would throw it at the servants stating that he wasn't hungry and accusing them of trying to poison him.

Then one day in 29 B.C. King Herod the Great called his Master of the House and ordered to get all the family together because they needed to have a family meeting. However, only his sister Salome, ex-Maccabim Queen Alexandra II and her daughter Mariamne I were invited. The three women entered the throne room and stood before the king. Queen Mariamne asked the king what the family meeting was about and that she had official business that was pressing. King Herod the Great smiled and answered, "Patience my Queen. I believe that my sister Salome has something to say." Salome stepped forward bowed her head and said, "Thank you my King. It saddens me and sickens me to report that your Queen Mariamne I has betrayed you." At this Mariamne I exclaimed, "What? You wicked witch!" Then King Herod the Great ordered, "Guards, restrain her!" Two big body guards seized Mariamne I and held her tight by both arms. Herod then looked directly at Mariamne I with a sly smile and said with false sympathy, "I am sorry for the inconsiderate interruption my faithful sister, please continue where you left off." Salome continued, "Thank you my gracious king. Your young queen, whom you have taken into your generous care and have given her all your dedicated love, has been caught being unfaithful to you. She has cheapened your love and dedication by sharing it with another man." Mariamne I could not control herself and screamed, "You lying witch. I should have your tongue cut out of that big mouth of yours!" Then one of the guards backhanded the Queen across the mouth and barked, "Silence!" A trickle of bright red blood began to flow down her chin from her bottom lip.

Then the ex-Maccabim Queen Alexandra II, the mother of Mariamne I said, "Great king if I may speak. My daughter has been trouble since the day she was born. Her father ex-king Alexander II and I presented her to you as a young bride in hopes she would someday learn to be grateful. I must apologize to you for her rude and un-lady like behavior today and the pathetic news of her disingenuous appreciation for everything that you have given to her." Her mother Alexandra II testified against her because she had learned that she too was on the hit list to be executed of King Herod the Great and wanted to save her own life. Then King Herod the Great spoke to Mariamne I, "Young woman you have shattered my heart today. This news of sharing your bed and my love with another man brings disgust to the sound of it to my very ears. Today according to law you will be bound and stoned to death as the justifiable punishment for wanton adultery. You have committed a crime against the king himself. Guards, get her out of my sight!" She immediately was led away to the pit of stoning. Queen Mariamne I Maccabim remained calm and serene at her execution at the age of twenty-five years old, having given birth to five children in the past seven years. The dark Vulture of Death filled its sharp beak with her innocent flesh and hovered over the Palace in Yruwshalaim (Jerusalem) as if expecting to be fed by the king.

The Vulture of Death was not to be disappointed. Two months later, ex-Queen Alexandra II complained to *Gadowl Kohen,* High Priest Pharisee Rabbi Yhowshuwa III that King Herod the Great was not mentally fit for the throne. Herod the Great found out and had her throat cut in a public execution for sedition against the throne. Then the very next year in 28 B.C. King Herod the Great executed his brother-in-law and father of Bernice, Kostobar for conspiracy in opposing the role that his wife, Herod's sister, Salome played in the deceitful trial of Mariamne I. The only constructive thing that King Herod the Great did that year when his paranoia was not corrupting his spirit was that he built a large theater and an amphitheatre for entertainment in the great city of Yruwshalaim (Jerusalem). Yhowshuwa III confronted King Herod the Great concerning all the executions of the royal family and made it very clear that he and the Sanhedrin were displeased and wanted them to cease immediately. Five years of bloodless peace were a welcome sight in the palace and the great city.

Early that fall of 23 B.C. as Prince Matityahu ben Levi was visiting his bachelor son, Prince Alexander III Helios, he informed his father that he would like to marry the teenage daughter, Chana (Hannah), of the *Gadowl Kohen*, High Priest, Yhowshuwa III, his neighbor across the street. Matityahu ben Levi was overjoyed that his bachelor son was finally getting married. He met with Pharisee Rabbi Yhowshuwa III and set a high dowry which would be paid in full fourteen months later by January of 21 B.C. when the *nesuin*, the final wedding ceremony would take place. This marriage would be important because it combined the *Gadowl Kohen*, High Priest Levitical bloodline of Aharown (Aaron) and the Davidic bloodline of King David, legal right to the throne of the Hebrews. This combination of High Priest and King had not been known since the days of Malkiy-Tsedeq (King of Righteousness) Melchizedek who did not have any lineage of beginning or record of his death but was king of Shalam, the City of Peace (Jerusalem) in the time of

Abraham two thousand and seventy years earlier. Therefore, the first male child of this marriage would have the legal right to be High Priest and King of the Hebrews as prophesied by the prophets of old. Thus, the youngest daughter of the *Gadowl Kohen*, High Priest Chana (Hannah) was betrothed to the bachelor prince 'Heli' ben Matityahu (Matthat). This was exciting news and all of the great city of Yruwshalaim (Jerusalem) was a buzz except for the Palace of Herod the Great who's paranoia summoned back the black Vulture of Death to prepare to feast with its sharp beak on the human flesh of the victim of his murderous plot.

Mid-summer of 23 B.C. King Herod the Great decided to marry his third wife, Mariamne II, the daughter of the Sadducee Rabbi *kohen*, priest, Simon IV ben Boethus. She was also the first cousin of *Gadowl Kohen*, High Priest, Yhowshuwa III. She was quite a bit younger than King Herod the Great and the High Priest let him know about it. Mariamne II changed her name to Herodes and after a couple of months played on the paranoia of the king in a power play for her father and the Sadducee Party. She riled up King Herod the Great against Pharisee Rabbi Yhowshuwa III to where the king believed in his mind that the *Gadowl Kohen*, High Priest was inciting the Sanhedrin to dethrone him, which was not true at all. So in the early fall of that year, King Herod the Great called Yhowshuwa III to the Herodian Palace for a special meeting. At that meeting, Queen Herodes spread deceitful lies about her first cousin and King Herod the Great removed Pharisee Rabbi Yhowshuwa (Joshua) III from all priestly duties in the Temple because of sedition against the throne and commanded him to go straight home. When Yhowshuwa III was three blocks from his home in the Upper City he was jumped by palace assassins and killed under the king's orders. That evening King Herod the Great announced to an emergency meeting of the

Sanhedrin that Sadducee Rabbi Simon IV Boethus, his new father-in-law was conferred the dignity of *Gadowl Kohen*, High Priest and that Pharisee Yhowshuwa III was killed by a band of robbers on his way home from a meeting at the palace.

Prince Alexander III Helios did his best to comfort his betrothed wife Chana (Hannah) and her mother. All of the great city of Yruwshalaim mourned and lamented for the gentle and honest *kohen*, priest, Yhowshuwa III. The great city was in grief when they laid the body of Yhowshuwa III in the *qeber*, sepulcher. It did not have to be spoken but the great city of Yruwshalaim (Jerusalem) knew that the 'butcher king' was responsible for this heinous death. After the burial, Prince Matityahu ben Levi came and stayed with his bachelor son while his wife Rachel of Arimathea stayed with the widow and daughter of Yhowshuwa III to help wherever she could. The outpouring of gifts and food was beyond belief as many who the family did not even know came to personally express their sorrow and even outrage that their 'favorite' *Gadowl Kohen*, High Priest had been murdered.

Emotionally the next fifteen months were very difficult for the Prince Heli and his betrothed bride Chana (Hanna). However, in January of 21B.C. the dark heavens got brighter as the pre-dawn light grew much larger and began coming much faster towards earth as Prince Heli and Chana stepped under the *chuppah*. This *chuppah* was very special because it did not contain any poles or a white decorated sheet. Two old friends of Yhowshuwa III, Matityahu ben Levi, the father of the groom and Yhowchanan Melek'Beyth (John Henry) Aer (Ayers) neighbor and fan-maker, held the prayer shawl of the bride's dead father above the couple as the *chuppah*. After the *nesiun*, wedding ceremony was complete, the prayer shawl was carefully folded and given to the wedding couple as a gift from dead Yhowshuwa III to his daughter, the bride.

The following year in 20 B.C. Prince Heli came rushing home from a business meeting in the Bezetha District of the great city of Yruwshalaim (Jerusalem). He burst through the door and panting said, "Anna, Anna! Where are you? I have amazing news." Chana (Hanna) called Prince Alexander III Helios by his nickname of Heli so he called her by her nickname of Anna. "*Man?*, What is it, Heli," she said coming from around the corner of the hallway. Heli continued, "Ol' King Herod the Great is going to spend some of his tax money that he has taken from the people and expand the Temple Mount by completely rebuilding the Temple of Yruwshalaim (Jerusalem). He is so proud of himself that he is even going to change the name from the Temple of Yahuah to Herod's Temple." Anna chimed in, "That old buzzard." Heli interrupted her, "Wait! Wait! That is not the best part. I have been chosen as the overseer of the construction project." Anna grabbed his neck in a big hug and said, "That is wonderful dear. I am so proud of you. My father would have been so proud of you too."

After a long embrace, Anna said, "Since the most pressing subject today is about recent construction projects, I have been looking at our house that your father left to us and have been thinking…." Heli interjected, "Now, Anna, this house is plenty big to have a family in, we don't need to be prideful and try to outdo King Herod by building a bigger house." Anna playfully stuck out her bottom lip like she used to do as a little girl and said, "It might be big enough but a little addition would bring you great joy." Heli once again stopped her, "I don't need any more rooms besides that is just that much more work for the servants to keep clean." Anna continued to tease her unsuspecting husband, "Oh, but dear all kings need a throne room and you are king of this castle. I was thinking about a jewel for your crown, my prince." Heli totally confused now quipped, "Anna, stop this nonsense! King Herod the Great would have me killed just like he did your father if he thought I was trying to be a king!"

Anna continued, "That is very true my prince. However, what if he could not see the addition and besides it has already begun and can't be stopped until completed, daddy." Now Prince Heli blew a gasket, "What? You are a woman and have no authority to order such a thing! The contractors must be halted and where is this construction happening? I must see it now!" Anna just giggled and replied, "I thought the mid-section would be most appropriate, daddy." Heli turned away from her and began walking to the center of the house muttering with each step, "I just don't know what possessed you to do this against my will. With all the new pressure of the Temple construction for the king and now my wife orders work to be done on my own house without…." He stopped mid-sentence and turned around as she was following him every step of the way and said, "Construction? Mid-section? Daddy? You mean I or I should say, we are going to have a baby?" She grabbed him in a tight embrace and said softly, "Yes, my prince, before the end of the year you will be holding your first child." Heli was so moved by the good news that tears began to slowly roll down his cheeks into his beard. Then in the first part of December the construction in the womb of Anna was complete and little Miryam (Mary) was born into this world of struggle between good and evil, Truth and lies, Yahuah Yahusha and Satan.

The great city of Yruwshalaim (Jerusalem) breathed a sigh of relief in 18 B.C. because King Herod the Great and his paranoia left the great city to visit Rome and Caesar Octavian Augustus. The tension in the air of having to watch over your shoulder constantly lifted as his royal caravan and entourage went through the western gates towards the port city of Yofa (Joppa) to catch the king's ship in order to sail to Rome. Anna also announced that year to Heli that eighteen month old Miryam (Mary) would become a big sister. Once again Prince Heli in early 17 B.C. fathered a very beautiful baby girl named Shalowmit (Salome). He loved coming home to spend time with 'his girls' after a long day at the Temple renovations. He worked so hard and the construction was five months ahead of schedule. The entire Sanhedrin praised him for a job well done as they even made suggestions according to the way Solomon's Temple used to look like. Heli was also a good manager as to this point in the construction he had saved twenty-one percent in projected costs. He knew this would please King Herod the Great because the king counted every penny.

Then in the very late fall before the winter rains came to the territory, shortly after the Feast of Tabernacles, King Herod the Great returned from Rome in a foul mood. When he saw some of the changes made by the Sanhedrin to make the Temple like the first one built by King Solomon he exploded and called Heli into the throne room. Heli expecting praise from the king and was taken aback when the king responded, "What has happened to my temple?" Heli replied, "Oh, great king, the Temple is five months ahead of construction schedule and I have saved twenty-one percent of projected costs for your treasury while you were gone to Rome." "While I was gone to Rome, you have gone behind my back and usurped my authority and changed my construction plans. Who gave you the authority to deviate from my original plans?" snorted Herod the Great. Heli tried to be calm and said, "My king, the only thing that was changed was some minor things in the interior of the Temple by the suggestion of the Sanhedrin to be like the great Temple of King Solomon." King Herod grew beet red and exploded, "Is this Herod's Temple or Solomon's Temple? Which king do you serve, a dead washed up king of the past or do I sit on the royal throne before your face at this moment? Whose crown do you see on my head?"

Then King Herod the Great stood up from sitting on the throne and pointed his index finger and shook it at Heli and continued, "It has come before my ears while I was in Rome that you are a prince from the tribe of Yhuwdah (Judah). Maybe you think you should be sitting in my place on the royal throne." Then the king gestured with his hand sweeping it towards the throne and said, "Go ahead the throne is empty, take it and see how it feels since you and your family want it so bad. You think you have the authority of the throne anyway and make decisions against my will and without respecting my authority. So go ahead and take my throne Prince Heli and make yourself king." Heli just froze not knowing how to respond to the paranoia of King Herod the Great. Then the king began his irate tirade again, "No matter whether you respond to me or not Prince Alexander Helios III, I am, King Herod the Great, who has the real authority of this throne, empty or if I am sitting on it, and I find your loyalty is devoted to a dead King Solomon instead of me. I, also find you guilty of trying to usurp my authority and place it upon yourself as king in my absence, trying to steal the throne away from me and my family and return it to the Davidic Dynasty. Ha ha, the joke is on you because King David is dead, King Solomon is dead and you are dead! Guards!!" Immediately, Eliy ben Matityahu (Prince Alexander Helios III) nicknamed Heli was seized, taken outside and beheaded on the orders of the 'Butcher King'.

Anna was mortified when she found out what had happened to her husband. It brought back horrific memories of when King Herod had assassinated her father the high priest. She collapsed in total grief and refused to be consoled. Prince Matityahu ben Levi, Heli's father rushed to Yruwshalaim as soon as word reached his ears. His wife Rachel of Arimathea did what she could once again to help comfort Anna but to no avail. The whole city was once again in shock and in terrifying fear as this news ran cold in the veins of communication throughout the great city. Everyone suspected someone and someone suspected everyone. Neighborly trust had evaporated and was replaced with suspecting treason to reach the paranoia ears of the king.

Matityahu ben Levi and Rachel decided to take Chana (Anna) back to the estates of Arimathea where her and her infant daughters, Miryam (Mary) and Shalowmit (Salome) would be safer. However, the Vulture of Death guided by the dark lord circled the Estates of Arimathea, far above the little village town of Ramah, waiting and watching for the next human flesh to feed his never satisfied belly of death and decay. Late in 15 B.C Rachel died during childbirth leaving Matityahu ben Levi with their newborn son, Yowceph (Joseph) ben Matityahu. The death of Rachel was too much and too soon for young Chana (Anna) and she died in early 14 B.C. leaving her now two orphaned daughters with Matityahu ben Levi to raise by himself in addition to his newborn son. This was just too much for the now aging Matityahu ben Levi so he took the two girls, his six-year old and four-year old granddaughters, to the unfinished Temple in the great city of Yruwshalaim (Jerusalem) to be raised within the Order of the Temple-Virgins until they were eligible for marriage after their bat-Mitzvoth, which was thirteen years old. Matityahu ben Levi bitterly sobbed all the way back home to the Estates of Arimathea in the little village of Ramah as his heart had literally been shattered by all this death and heartache. Only the innocence of his newborn son kept him striving to remain alive.

Also, that year in 14 B.C., Ya'kov Melek'Beyth Aer (James Henry Ayers) the fan maker became the father of Chizqiy (Charles) meaning strong. He was a beautiful baby but his lungs were weak and he wheezed a lot. As his mother nursed him she would also put a mixture of the sticky-gummy syrup of honey and finely ground cinnamon on his tongue which seemed to help his breathing. He was seventh in a line of twelve children to be born into this family. Also, in the great city Sadducee Rabbi Sethus ben Boethus, who was also called Yhowshuwa (Joshua) IV, the uncle of martyr Pharisee Rabbi Yhowshuwa (Joshua) III, fathered a son named Chananyah (Ananias) ben Sethus. Sadducee Rabbi Sethus ben Boethus took over as the *Gadowl Kohen*, High Priest from his brother, Simon IV, the father-in-law of King Herod the Great in 19 B.C. and served in this powerful capacity until 4 B.C. Matityahu ben Levi was reminded of all the death that surrounded his family each time he looked at something at the Estates of Arimathea. Therefore, he packed up a few of the servants and took his infant son Yowceph (Joseph) ben Matityahu of Arimathea and moved north to the territory of Galiylah (Galilee) to the small quiet village of Nazareth. His new neighbor across the street was the carpenter Ya'aqob (Jacob) ben El'azar who also had a young son named Yowceph (Joseph). Matityahu ben Levi continued to manage the family mining business from this quiet little village of Nazareth and also kept tabs on the Estates in Arimathea.

For the next four years leading to 10 B.C. the mental illness of King Herod the Great grew beyond paranoia and his disease was taken out on his royal family. In 13 B.C. King Herod made his first-born son with his first wife Doris, Antipater as first heir in his will which only seemed right as he was the oldest of Herod's sons. Then in 12 B.C. King Herod's paranoia suspected both of his sons from the marriage of Mariamne I, Alexander and Aristobulus of trying to threaten his life. He took both of them to the northern town of Aquileia, Italy to be imprisoned and tried with a death sentence but Caesar Octavian Augustus reconciled the three. King Herod the Great then amended his will to include Alexander and Aristobulus but Atipater would be the highest in the succession to the throne. Before King Herod the Great left Rome and Caesar Octavian Augustus, the king gave heavy support and almost single handily financed the strapped Olympic Games. Then in 10 B.C. King Herod the Great inaugurated the newly expanded temple in the great city of Yruwshalaim (Jerusalem) calling it 'Herod's Temple'. Now that the king had his own temple he could be a god of power like Caesar in Rome.

The paranoia and depression of King Herod the Great compounded into a physical sickness appropriately called "Herod's Evil". The pain was excruciating the final years of his life. He had chronic kidney disease complicated by Fournier's gangrene. He also had scabies with visible worms crawling in his putrefied decaying flesh. His spiritual health was even worse as he wanted to be worshiped as a god giving his spirit over to the control of demonic activity. Thus the disease of Herod the Great grew more severe each year and he cursed Yahuah blaming Him for inflicting punishment on him for his crimes.

A slow fire burned within him which was not so apparent to those who were in touch with him, but augmented his internal distress; for he had a terrible desire for food which it was not possible to resist. He was also affected with ulceration of the intestines with especially severe pain in the colon, while watery and transparent tumors settled about his feet and abdomen. He became morbidly overweight and had to have a much larger throne built to hold his massive body. The king also had trouble breathing and the odor of his breath was overwhelming. He suffered from convulsions in every limb which gave him uncontrollable strength. King Herod the Great literally became a demonic beast imprisoned by a human body of decaying flesh and bone.

The dark lord Satan was pleased with the progress that he and his bestial minions had accomplished on the face of the earth. The dark lord was in control of the largest and most powerful government on the face of the earth known as the Roman Empire. Caesar Octavian Augustus considered himself immortal being a 'son of a god' and worshiped the dark lord through idolatry and the Imperial Cult. The dark lord also had full mental, physical and spiritual control over the most powerful king in one of Rome's territories. King Herod the Great, the king over the people of Yahuah could not think or move without full control of the dark lord Satan. The Sanhedrin was tired of the 'Butcher King' but dared not to oppose him. The Sadducee Party supported the king as long as he stayed out of the temple business but the Pharisee Party politically and spiritually opposed his throne and actively searched out a Davidic Prince of the tribal branch of Yhuwdah to regain the royal throne.

The Hebrew people in the territory of Yhuwdah (Judea) lived in extreme fear, the citizens of the great city of Yruwshalaim (Jerusalem) dwelt in extreme fear, the servants and staff in the Palace of Herod served in great fear and the family of King Herod the Great daily trembled and walked in fear for their lives. As a matter of fact, Caesar Octavian Augustus knew what dire circumstances that the family members surrounding King Herod the Great lived under once said as he tried to make a joke of the situation, "It is preferable to be Herod's pig (*hus* in the Greek language) than his son (*huios* in the Greek language)." Of course this remark was an extreme insult to all Hebrews but none the less King Herod the Great thought it was funny when the joking statement finally reached his ears. This reaction to Caesar's joke sent chills down the spines of all his sons who were vying for the throne of their dying father the king. The coal black Vulture of Death drooled with salvia as he saw the weakening king ready to 'butcher' anyone for any reason at any time. The only thing that kept the king alive was the determination that maybe before the sun would set on the next day he could find just one little thing that would give him a reason to murder his three oldest sons. A pitch black thick cloud of dark wickedness began forming over the great city of Yruwshalaim and the territory of Yhuwdah. A cloud of uncomforting fear and a deep sense of hopelessness began to shadow the thoughts and lives of all who dwelt in this demonic controlled community. The prayers of the faithful intensified as they needed a shimmering beacon of light to make this cloud of darkness flee back to its master.

16

The last B.C. decade continued to be filled with royal intrigue fueled by the mental and physical illness of King Herod the Great. In 8 B. C. King Herod once again accused his sons Alexandros and Aristobulus from Mariamne I Maccabim of high treason. Caesar Octavian Augustus gave him permission to proceed legally against his sons. Therefore in 7 B.C. the court hearing took place in Berytos (Beirut, Lebanon) before a Roman court and the sons of Mariamne I were found guilty and executed. Now the succession to the throne of King Herod the Great changed so that Antipater, the oldest son, who was from the first marriage of Doris, is the exclusive successor to the throne. In second place the succession to the royal throne of King Herod incorporated Herod Philip, the son of Mariamne II, King Herod's third wife.

Things seemed to be going King Herod's way until in 6 B.C. the Pharisees announced to King Herod that a Messiah would come and take away his throne and end his barbaric rule. King Herod the Great mentally exploded and began intense persecutions on all the Pharisees claiming to be from the priestly line of Tsadaq (Zadok) and any Hebrew who claimed to be from the Davidic lineage. He even suspected his oldest son Antipater and brought him before the court and charged him with the intended murder of the king. However, King Herod the Great first needed the approval granted only by a Roman emperor to enforce the death penalty. While he was seeking approval of Caesar Octavian Augustus, he once again changed his will so that Herod Antipas from his fourth marriage with Malthace, as the successor to his throne. Caesar Octavian Augustus approved the death penalty request and King Herod the Great executed his oldest son Antipater in 5 B.C.

With all the astonishment going on with the palace intrigue of the 'Butcher King', the world seemed to forget about two orphaned princesses living at the Order of the Temple-Virgins. Late in 7 B.C. Princess Miryam (Mary) had her bat-Mitzvoth so she wrote to her grandfather Matityahu ben Levi who was living in the small village Nazareth in the territory of Galiylah (Galilee) asking him to come get her and betroth her to marriage and she would be responsible for her younger sister, Princess Shalowmit (Salome). One week later Matityahu ben Levi arrived at the Order of the Temple-Virgins to get his grown up teenage granddaughters.

Miryam (Mary) and Shalowmit (Salome) mounted the donkeys as they followed their grandfather out of the great city of Yruwshalaim (Jerusalem). Then Matityahu ben Levi said, "Girls, your aunt Elysheba (Elizabeth) and I had been talking and we thought it would be a good idea if you two stayed with her a couple of months in the hill country. As you know the poor thing is barren and it would be nice of you two if you could fill that empty place in her heart while I make the final arrangements for you to come live with me in Nazareth." Then Miryam said, "But grandfather what about my betrothal?" Matityahu ben Levi replied, "I am working on that too. I have been talking to the carpenter Ya'aqob ben El'azar who has a handsome son named Yowceph and…" Miryam interrupted with a hint of disgust, "A carpenter! Really grandfather, is he the only man available?" Matityahu ben Levi continued, "Now, wait a minute Miryam don't judge so quickly. This is not just any carpenter but he is the one that made that beautiful chest that has your belongings in it behind you on the pack mule. If I remember right, when you saw that chest you remarked and I quote, '*What a beautiful expensive chest. You shouldn't have grandfather.*' Unquote." Shalowmit burst out laughing as her sister Miryam blushed and quickly back-stepped saying, "Well an exquisite carpenter might have advantageous qualities." Matityahu ben Levi said laughing, "Granddaughter you definitely have the spunk of your mother in you, Yahuah rest her soul." Then the small caravan continued to ride into the hill country as the girls chattered about Aunt Elysheba.

As they neared their house, Uncle Rabbi Zkaryah (Zacharias) and Aunt Elysheba (Elizabeth) came jogging down the dusty road to meet them as they frantically waved their arms in excited greetings shouting, "Shalowm, shalowm!" They met in the middle of the dusty road as Elysheba said, "Oh, I am so glad you girls came. I think you have grown a foot since we saw you at the Temple during the Feast of Weeks (Pentecost) a couple months ago." Matityahu ben Levi greeted Rabbi Zkaryah, "Shalowm brother, I hope all is well with you." Rabbi Zkaryah acknowledged grinning from ear to ear, "Fine, fine, all is fine." Then Elysheba said, "Zkaryah would you just look at how big these girls have gotten since we saw them at the Temple." Zkaryah replied, "*Ken, ken*, yes, yes Elysheba I can see. Now hurry inside and finish fixing something to eat. It will be sundown soon and I bet everyone is hungry and thirsty. Why, that trip from the great city Yruwshalaim can really make your throat a desert." They all settled down inside the house for a great meal and fellowship for the evening. The next morning Matityahu ben Levi left to return home to Galiylah (Galilee) to the little town of Nazareth while the girls stayed and helped their Aunt Elysheba (Elizabeth) until their grandfather's return.

Two months later as promised just before the seven day celebration of the Feast of Tabernacles, which required Uncle Zkaryah (Zacharias) to travel to the Temple in Yruwshalaim, grandfather Matityahu ben Levi retured to the hill country to fetch the girls and take them both home with him to the small town of Nazerath. As usual before Matityahu ben Levi could get to the house, Elysheba (Elizabeth) came trotting down the dusty road waving her arms frantically and jumped up and down with excitement and joy yelling, "Girls! Girls! He has come. Your grandfather has come. Miryam (Mary) and Shalowmit (Salome) hurry and come see." Then came calm Uncle Zkaryah muttering, "Now wife, don't work yourself into a tissy. Everyone can see Matityahu coming, maybe even the dead has heard you." Elysheba paid Zkaryah no mind and joyfully escorted Matityahu ben Levi to the house and with the help from the two girls began to prepare a big meal for the evening.

After a good nights rest and warm food in their full bellies, Matityahu and the girls headed home to the small village of Nazareth where the gossip mill was working anticipating having two princesses coming to live in their little village with their wealthy grandfather and young eight-year old step-uncle Yowceph of Arimathea. When they got to Nazareth the people were outside their houses and businesses waving and mostly gawking with curiosity. However, when they got to their house, a very handsome young man stood across the street with a carpenter's apron tied around his waist with his arms folded across his chest, and leanning against the doorway. Miryam (Mary) quickly said to her grandfather Matityahu, "Who is that handsome man across the street?" Matityahu ben Levi answered teasingly, "Oh never mind him. He is Yowceph (Joseph) the *ben,* son, of a lowly carpenter. The very one who's hands built that beautiful chest of yours that you like so much. However, remember, carpenters are beneath your desire for a husband?" Then twelve-year old Shalowmit burst into the conversation, "Grandfather, if Miryam does not want him can I have him?" Matityahu turned towards Shalowmit (Salome) and said, "I must keep that in mind." This reply brought both arms on Miryam's hips with disdain after she quickly dismounted her donkey and with a scolding voice said, "Sister you just need to be silent and grandfather you can't be serious? How could you do that to me since I am the oldest?" Then grandfather Matityahu looked to heaven and exclaimed, "*Oy vey*, Oh pain, Yahuah. Boys are so much easier." Then shaking his head back and forth as he tied up the three donkeys, he took the girls inside the house and introduced them to their step-uncle Yowceph (Joseph) of Arimathea. He showed them to their room that the two girls would share and told them that the cook would call them when the evening meal was prepared and it was time to eat. The two teenage girls doted over their eight-year old uncle, their dead father's half-brother, and the three bonded very easily. The girls even learned their house responsibilities very quicky and eagerly did them.

During the next year, 6 B.C. Matityahu ben Levi negotiated with Ya'aqob (Jacob) ben El'azar on the dowry for the betrothal of Princess Miryam (Mary) to Yowceph (Joseph), the carpenter son of Ya'aqob ben El'azar. The proposed groom had two years to raise the dowry to complete the agreement. Miryam glowed with satisfaction and joy and increased her natural yearning for the Torah and the writings of the prophets. She watched her proposed groom from the women's section in the local synagogue and noticed with satisfaction that Yowceph eagerly participated in the discussions and that he worshiped with his whole being during the service to Yahuah. After each service he would turn and fix his gaze into the eyes of Miryam and simply smile. Each smile would bring a blush to the cheeks of Miyram and jab of a finger and giggle from her sister Shalowmit.

The bright pre-dawn light was now almost unbearable to the

demonic mass of darkness attempting to block it from shining upon the face of the earth. Its power seemed to be unstoppable and its rays of light burned the evil bodies of the minions of Satan. The lieutenant commanders could not any longer control their ranks and chaos ensued with the constant whimpering and cries of pain as the evil minions tried to shield their red-glowing eyes from the pure bright rays of light. Their sharp talons clawed each other as the front lines quickly retreated from the blinding light as the power of evil darkness surrendered to the coming pre-dawn light. A beacon of light shot rapidly towards the face of the earth as it pierced through the unorganized ranks of the dark evil minions.

During the month of Tammuz (June-July) in 5 B.C. *Kohen*, priest, Zkaryah (Zacharias) had to leave his wife Elysheba (Elizabeth) in the hill country and serve in the Temple in the great city of Yruwshalaim (Jerusalem). His Levitical order of service was from the clan of the descendents of Abiyah and served the Temple in the eighth and thirty-second week of service according to the lunar (moon) year as commanded in the First book of *Divrei Hayyamim*, Spoken Words of the Matters of the Days (Chronicles). He was also required to be in Yruwshalaim to serve in the Temple three other times of the year as set by the Torah book of *Dabar*, Spoken Words (Deuteronomy). This additional service which did not count in the number of the weekly service schedules, were the celebrations of *Pecach/Matstsah Lechem*, Passover/Unleavened Bread; *Chamishshiym*, Feast of Weeks (Pentecost); and *Cukkah*, Feast of Tabernacles. Thus Zkaryah was required to travel the long dusty road to the great city of Yruwshalaim (Jerusalem) five times during the lunar (new moon) year which began in the month of Nisan (late March-early April) as set by the Torah book of *Elleh Shem*, These Were the Names (Exodus).

Therefore, during the ninth week of the lunar year, the order of the descendents of Abiyah served the Temple and it was during the service of Zkaryah (Zacharias) of his performing his functions as the *kohen*, officiating priest in the fixed succession of regular arrangement of his daily shift in front of Yahuah according to the law of the function of priests, his lot was to fumigate with smoking aromatic fumes as he entered into the Most Sacred Place of the Temple of Yahuah. As he went behind the Sacred Curtain, a large crowd of people prayed to Yahuah at that very hour of the aroma from the fragrant burnt powder. Then all of a sudden a beacon of bright light flashed before his eyes and there stood a magnificent messenger angel standing in front of him on the right side of the Altar of Incense. Zkaryah was seized with great fear as he gazed with wide open eyes the messenger angel.

Then the messenger angel said in a booming voice, "Do not be frightened Zkaryah, I am Gabriy'Yah (Gabriel) bringing you tidings from Yahuah. Your petition was listend to and your wife Elysheba will give birth to a son for you and you will call his name Yowchanan (John). He will be a delight and exultation to you and many will be happy and cheerful over his nativity. It is for this reason. He will be great in the eyes of Yahuah and he shall not at all drink any wine or intensely fermented liquor. He will be filled with the influence of the Sacred Breath even from his mother's womb cavity of the matrix. He will turn back one hundred and eighty degrees the hearts of many of the sons of Yisra'Yah (Israel) to their Master, Yahuah. Your son will precede as a forerunner of Him, the Messiah, in the breath and miraculous power of the prophet Eliyah (Elijah) to make ready a righteous people for Yahuah Yahusha."

Then Zkaryah said to Gabriy'Yah, "By what will I know this? I exist as an old man and my wife is advanced in years in her days." The messenger angel Gabriy'Yah (Gabriel) responded and said to him, "I exist as Gabriy'Yah, the one standing in front of the face of Yahuah. I was sent on a mission to talk to you and to announce the good news of these things to you. Thus, you will be hushed and mute and not able to utter words until which the day that these things come into being because you did not have faith in what I said, which will verify the prediction in their set and proper time." Then in an instant the glowing figure of the messenger angel Gabriy'Yah disappeared and Zkaryah (Zacharias) was all alone in the Most Holy Place.

Some of the people who were in the court of men praying were in admiration of Zkaryah lingering and taking his time in the Most Holy Place of the Temple while others anticipated in hope that he would soon appear fearing that he died in the presence of Yahuah. When he finally appreard from behind the Sacred Curtain he was not able to talk to them and they became fully acquainted with that he had experienced clearly and stared at a vision in the Temple. They peppered him with many questions and he was nodding and expressing by signs waving across space but he stayed constantly mute and no one could figure out what he was trying to tell them. Even though it was the end of his weekly service he could not be released to go home because the following week (week ten of the lunar year) was *Chamishshiym*, Feast of Weeks (Pentecost) the second of three mandatory feast attendance by all *kohens*, priests. Zkaryah (Zacharais) was released to go back home to his wife Elysheba at the beginning of week eleven of the lunar year.

Zkaryah hurried back to the hill country to try to explain to his wife Elysheba (Elizabeth) about the visit of the messenger angel Gabriy" Yah (Gabriel) in the Temple. He could not wait to tell her that she soon would be pregnant. Actually he could not tell her since he was mute but he could draw it out on paper or in the dirt. Not only could Zkaryah not speak he could not get Elysheba pregnant for two more weeks because she had just begun her cycle flow for seven days. Then according to the laws of impurity in the Torah book of *Vayiqra*, Yahuah Called (Leviticus), as a *kohen*, priest he could not be around blood, except only the sacrifices at the Temple, so he had to wait seven days by Law after her blood flow stopped. But during the thirteenth week of the lunar year, he was able to know his wife and she conceived just as Gabriy'Yah (Gabriel) had predicted.

Twenty-five and a half weeks later in the same year of 5 B.C. in the sixth new moon (month) of Tevet (December-January) Miryam (Mary) was in her room daydreaming of her betrothal and the gentle smiles of Yowceph (Joseph) after each synagogue. Tonight would be a special synagogue service as it was the historical celebration of 25th of Kislev (November-December). On this day of each year was a celebration for eight consecutive days for the Feast of Dedication called *Chanukah*, Hanukkah. It was also known as the Festival of Lights. It was an especially important day to Miryam (Mary) because it was her Maccabim bloodline that began this special Festival of Lights some one-hundred and fifty-nine years earlier. Her daydreaming was interrupted by the crackling voice of the cook yelling, "Miryam, Miryam girl. Do you hear me? Hurry and get the goat milked because sunset will be here soon. You don't want to miss *Chanukah*, Hanukkah at the synagogue tonight do you?" Miryam bolted up and ran out of her room and out of the house towards the goat shed in the back. She quickly grabbed the bucket and swung it in front of her as she entered inside the shed.

The nanny goat did not like to be milked by her and it was always a battle of wits. Therefore she was always careful to get the door behind her shut securely or else the nanny goat would escape into the backyard. Miryam dropped the small pail by her feet, put her hands on her hips and took a deep breath scolding, "Alright, Miss Nanny, I don't have time to mess with you tonight. It is a special synagogue for *Chanukah*, Hanukkah and I want to look nice when Yowceph (Joseph) smiles at me after service." Beams of faint light filtered through the cracks in the wood siding and the thatch roof overhead. Nanny Goat shook her head and bleated in a low 'I dare you' tone. Miryam took one step forward towards Miss Nanny and the goat pawed the earthen floor. Miryam stopped and shook her index finger at the goat saying, "Ok. So that is the way you want to do this, huh? If you would just cooperate this would all be over in a split second without all the fuss and muss." At this Miss Nanny bolted to the far corner of the small shed. Miryam tried to be quick to head the goat off but she tripped over the pail that she had put down at her feet when she had entered the shed. The sound of the kicked pail and the sight of Miryam (Mary) falling and rolling to the ground startled Miss Nanny and she ran to the wooden door.

Then the entire small shed was filled with a blinding light and a booming voice said, "Be well, the one endued with the special honor of grace. Yahuah is with you." Miryam, who was sitting up by now was alarmed at the sight of the glowing messenger angel and thoroughly reckoned and deliberated in her mind what kind of greeting this could be. The messenger angel continued, "I am Gabriy'Yah (Gabriel). Do not be frightened Miryam because you have found the divine influence of gratitude of the heart of Yahuah. Soon you will conceive in the matrix of your stomach and give birth to a Son and you will call his name, Yahusha. This One will be great and will be called the Son of Yahuah and Master Yahuah will give Him the throne of His father, David. He will rule over the family of Yisra'Yah (Israel) to the age of the Messianic period and His royalty, realm and rule will not have a conclusion." Miryam (Mary) questioned Gabriy'Yah (Gabriel), "How will this be sicne I have not known a man intimately?" The messenger angel responded and said to her, "The Sacred Breath (Holy Spirit) will supervene upon you and the miraculous power of Yahuah will envelope you in a haze of brilliant light so even that Regeneration will be called Sacred and Blameless, the consecrated Son of Yahuah. Even now your Aunt Elysheba (Elizabeth) has also conceived a son in her senility and she is in her sixth month, the one called cursed and sterile, because everything with Yahuah is not impossible." Then Miryam said, "I exist as a female slave of Yahuah. May it come into being to me according to your utterance."

Then Gabriy'Yah the messenger angel who was sent out on a mission by Yahuah to the northern territory of Galiylah (Galilee) to a small village town of Nazareth to deliver good tidings, departed from Miryam. The little wooden shed was once again darkened with only the small streams of dust filled light shining through the slats of the siding and cracks in the thatched roof. Miss Nanny, the goat, layed by the door at peace chewing her cud. Miyram sat there stunned for a while, then stood up and brushed herself off. She looked around the semi-dark shed and felt her head all around to see if she had hit it on something. Was what just happened real or was it a dream? Miss Nanny was not alarmed and seemed at peace. As Miryam looked closer, the little pail was standing upright. When she bent down to fetch it so that she could milk Miss Nanny and then go tell Grandfather Matityahu ben Levi and her sister Shalowmit (Salome) what had happened, she noticed something strange. The pail was full of milk! She thought silently, *"My eyes are playing tricks on me. What did Miss Nanny do to me?"*

The evil minions of Satan could no longer hold back the powerful light as their bodies screamed in pain with every move from the burning sensation of the pure brilliance. The large black scales on their cold-blooded bodies could no longer protect them. They howled and screamed with all their might to express their agony of pain to their heartless and unsympathetic commanders. Those who refused to move were hurled towards the light and their bestial bodies exploded in flames and instantly turned to ash with a crackling sound of lightning. Their once thick wall of evil darkness was now paper thin and the powerful rushing pre-dawn light of brilliance began to split open a gaping hole through their ranks to make its way to the face of the earth.

Then the head lieutenant commander yelled, "Who are you and what do you want? We will not surrender or bow to anyone but the dark lord, Satan! You will not claim victory over us today! I command you to show yourself and fight!" Then a thunderous voice shook the darkness and said, "I Exist that I Exist. I am Yahuah Yahusha, Creator of the heavens and the earth!" Then all the evil minions of Satan cowered and shook with fear and bowed their heads and knees as the powerful blinding pre-dawn Light passed by them in a mighty gust of blowing wind with a roaring thunderous sound.

Miryam stared at the full pail of milk and then looked at the peaceful goat, Miss Nanny. Now she didn't dare tell anyone about this expecially her little step-uncle Yowceph of Arimathea. He would tell Yowceph the carpenter after the service tonight and she would be the laughing stock of the little village town of Nazareth. What was she to do? Then a mighty gust of wind blew open the wooden door to the goat shed with a roaring thunderous sound and a powerful blinding light of the miraculous power of Yahuah enveloped Miryam (Mary) in a haze and she slowly crumpled unconscious to the floor of sod and....

"Unseen Footsteps of Jesus"
OLAM
HABA
(Future World)
Jerry Ayers

"Unseen Footsteps of Jesus"
OLAM
HABA
Mysteries Book 2- "The Dawning"
Jerry Ayers

"Unseen Footsteps of Jesus"
OLAM
HABA
(Future World)
Jerry Ayers

OLAM
HABA
(Future World)
Jerry Ayers

"Unseen Footsteps of Jesus"
OLAM
HABA
Jerry Ayers

"Unseen Footsteps of Jesus"
OLAM
HABA
(Future World)
Jerry Ayers

"Unseen Footsteps of Jesus"
OLAM
HABA
(Future World)
Jerry Ayers

OLAM
HABA
Jerry Ayers